THE
SAINTS' GUIDE
TO HAPPINESS

'Neither preachy nor potty, this charming exploration of the practice of happiness is a small gem.'
Salley Vickers, author of *Miss Garnet's Angel*

'Even when they suffer, the saints are happy. How is that possible? This delightful book comes as close as any to explaining it. But it isn't a book of explanations; it is a book that gently takes you on a journey into the world of practical wisdom. If you are searching for happiness, for life in abundance, you will not be disappointed.'
Stratford Caldecott, Chesterton Institute for Faith & Culture, Oxford

'Happiness is an elusive creature that can escape pursuit for a lifetime. Robert Ellsberg tells the stories of real people who have found it while learning how to work and to be still, to love and to be fully alive.'
Christopher Howse, editor of *The Best Spiritual Reading Ever*

'Happiness – deep, true, stable, lasting – is not the result of feelings, but is a by-product of holiness. Whatever the common opinion, it is in fact the holy who live life to the full. Robert Ellsberg understands this lovely paradox and explains all its implications with grace and charm.'
Sister Wendy Beckett, author of *Sister Wendy's Book of Saints*

'Books that promise painless enlightenment sit side-by-side with those that offer a lengthy practice too daunting to learn. *The Saints' Guide to Happiness* is neither. Robert Ellsberg has sifted through the wisdom of "those who walk the path of holiness" and produced neither a quick-fix nor a stiff tome, but a modern, refreshing guide to a true life and the kind of happiness that lasts.'
Nora Gallagher, author of *Practicing Resurrection*

'It takes a gifted writer to engage readers in a book of insights from men and women commonly understood to have spent their lives so close to God that they were unusual in almost every way. In this eloquent, seamlessly woven and delightfully readable book, Ellsberg makes the spiritual struggles and triumphs of sanctified men and women accessible and relevant.'
Pubishers Weekly

'Robert Ellsberg regards saints as friends worth knowing. His engaging book shows us why we should commune with the saints: for their uncommon wisdom as people who discovered that happiness and holiness are the same thing.'
Kenneth L. Woodward, author of *Making Saints*

THE
SAINTS' GUIDE
TO HAPPINESS

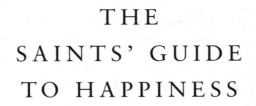

ROBERT ELLSBERG

Darton, Longman and Todd

First published in Great Britain in 2004 by
Darton, Longman and Todd Ltd
1 Spencer Court
140–142 Wandsworth High Street
London SW18 4JJ

First published in the USA in 2003 by
North Point Press
a division of Farrar, Straus and Giroux
19 Union Square West
New York 10003
USA

ISBN 0 232 52543 9

A catalogue record for this book is available from the British Library.

Designed by Jonathan D. Lippincott
Printed and bound in Great Britain by
The Cromwell Press, Trowbridge, Wiltshire

To Peggy

Cor ad cor loquitor

CONTENTS

PREFACE

For we are made for happiness, and any one who is completely happy has a right to say to himself, "I am doing God's will on earth." All the righteous, all the saints, all the holy martyrs were happy.
—Dostoevsky, *The Brothers Karamazov*

DEEP IN THE HEART of every person there is a longing for happiness. We may seek it by various routes and under different guises, as often as not illusory, but it is the same goal. It is the reason why people get married and why some get divorced, why some people set out on journeys, or buy lotto tickets, or study the stock market, or watch *Celebrity Fear Factor*. As Pascal noted, "The reason why some go to war and some do not is the same desire in both, but interpreted in two different ways. . . . This is the motive of every act of every person, including those who go and hang themselves."

But what *is* happiness? That is a universal question, as old as philosophy. More than fifteen hundred years ago, St. Augustine cited a scholar who could imagine as many as 288 possible schools of thought, depending on the various permutations in their approach to this subject. No doubt the intervening centuries have extended this tally.

"The pursuit of happiness" (a phrase enshrined in the Declaration of Independence) is the subject of innumerable books, even those ostensibly concerned with other topics. Many of them outline specific steps to follow—"Five Principles," "Nine Strategies," or even "100 Secrets"—for achieving this goal. Some of these books clearly identify happiness with "success," whether that is defined in terms of material prosperity or psychological well-being. Others explore the spiritual dimensions of happiness, emphasizing an attitude of awareness or virtues such as gratitude and forgiveness. Among the books in this category, a sizable number are by Buddhists. Even the Dalai Lama has contributed to this literature with his bestseller *The Art of Happiness*.

But even before we read any of these books, our imagination of happiness has been shaped by a constant stream of cultural messages. It is not just the magazine articles that promise happiness through better sex, a more youthful appearance, or a higher return on our investments. In virtually every advertisement and television commercial we confront people whose beatific expression exclaims, "This way lies happiness!"—if only we could have what they have, look more like them, be more like them.

What all these approaches have in common is a tendency to identify the pursuit of happiness in subjective terms. Happiness is ultimately a matter of *feeling* happy. But feelings are notoriously unstable, subject to a host of circumstances and influences beyond our control. This fact is reflected in the very etymology of the English word. "Happiness" derives from *hap*, a word meaning "chance" or "luck," as in "happen" or "happenstance."

But what if happiness is not subjective, a question of how we feel, or a matter of chance, something that simply *happens*? What if it is more like an *objective* condition, something analogous to bodily health? Aristotle took this view. The word he used for happiness, *eudaimonia*, is not a matter of feelings but a way of *being*, a certain fullness of life. Happiness, for Aristotle, has to do with living in accordance with the rational and moral order of the universe. It is more like the *flourishing* of a healthy plant than like Freud's pleasure principle. Because it is rooted in habits of the soul, it is the fruit of considerable striving. But for the same reason it is not subject to the vagaries of fortune.

The Greek-writing authors of the New Testament did not use Aristotle's word for happiness. They drew on another word, *makarios*, which refers to the happiness of the gods in Elysium. In the Gospel of Matthew this is the word that Jesus uses to introduce his Sermon on the Mount: "Happy are the poor in spirit. . . . Happy are the meek. . . . Happy are they who mourn. . . ." St. Jerome, who prepared the Latin translation in the fourth century, used *beatus*, a word that combines the connotations of being happy and blessed. Hence these verses are known as the Beatitudes. Forced to choose, most English translators have opted—probably wisely—for the more familiar "Blessed are . . ." The Beatitudes, after all, are not about "smiley faces" or feeling happy. They are not about feelings at all. They are about sharing in the life and spirit—the happiness—of God. In that spirit a disciple (like Jesus himself) could experience mourning, suffering, and loss while remaining "blessed"—happy, that is, in the most fundamental sense.

It is surprising, in this light, that Christians are so reluctant to address this topic. Why is this? Perhaps the pursuit of happiness seems vain or self-centered. The gospel, after all, is about salvation, not about success or "feeling good." On the other hand, there are many people who associate Christianity with grim moralism and self-denial; the Christian tradition is the last place they would seek advice about happiness. And so all these people, both Christians and those only tangentially related to any religious practice, remain unaware that the theme of happiness runs like a silver thread throughout the Christian tradition, especially in the wisdom of its prime exponents, those holy men and women known as saints.

In the light of popular conceptions of Christianity this statement may seem not simply unfamiliar but odd. Saints are surely experts on holiness, but what do they know about happiness? That depends, of course, on what we mean by happiness. But it also depends on our understanding of holiness. Saints, we may suppose, were flawless people from long ago who performed miracles, spent their lives in church, and eagerly sought opportunities to suffer agonizing and untimely deaths. To the extent that this describes our image of holy people—an image reflected all too often in stained-glass windows and holy cards—the wisdom of the saints appears both out of reach and off-putting. As a result, we may assume that Christianity has little relevance in answering the deepest yearnings of our hearts.

But as we learn more about the saints, we find that they pursued questions not unlike our own: What is the meaning and purpose of life? Why do so many of our hopes and plans end in sadness and disappointment? How can we find true peace? Is there a kind of happiness immune to loss, pain, and changing circumstances?

Many saints are well known: St. Augustine, St. Francis of

Assisi, St. Thomas Aquinas, or St. Teresa of Ávila. Others are obscure. Some of them died as martyrs (literally "witnesses") or devoted their lives to prayer and service of their neighbors. A few were even credited with miracles while they lived. But in the end they were not called saints because of the way they died, or because of their visions or wondrous deeds, but because of their extraordinary capacity for love and goodness, which reminded others of the love of God.

The lives of the saints, like our own, were often marked by suffering and hardship. If the saint's version of happiness meant being eaten by lions or wearing a hair shirt, it would likely attract few takers. But it is a mistake to identify saints with hardship and misery. In general they were renowned for their balance and good humor, their compassion and generosity, their spirit of peace and freedom in the face of obstacles and adversities, and their ability to find joy in all things. Such qualities made them, in many cases, the object not only of veneration but also of wonder and desire on the part of their contemporaries.

By the same token, it is a mistake to think of saints simply as figures from long ago. They are everywhere in our midst. Some of them are exceptional figures like Dorothy Day, Thomas Merton, Oscar Romero, or Mother Teresa. Others may be people we know or pass every day: people who remind us of God; people whose love, courage, and inner balance seem to set them apart—not above ordinary humanity, but as a standard of what human beings ought to be. When we are with such people, we come away feeling gladder, more grateful to be alive, perhaps wishing that we knew the "secret" of their inner illumination.

No saint ever composed a "guide to happiness." In fact many of them deliberately warned against the temptation to reduce the gospel to a system of techniques or "easy steps." As St. John of the Cross observed, there are those who "can never have enough of listening to counsels and learning spiritual precepts, and of possessing and reading many books which treat of this matter." The saints would have us remember that there is a great difference between the practice of holiness and simply reading lots of books "which treat of this matter."

With that warning, I offer in the following chapters an exploration of happiness through the lives and writings of various holy Christians. In effect my aim is to see what we might learn from such men and women about the meaning of a whole and authentic life. What lessons might they provide in the pursuit of happiness? How can they help us on the path to our true and best selves?

The sequence of these lessons follows an intuitive more than rational order. Any one of these chapters might be an entry into the wisdom of the saints and the opening to our own journey. In an actual life, of course, these themes are interwoven. Nevertheless, there is a certain arc that follows the progress from our earliest steps to our last.

The pursuit of happiness, often enough, begins with the initial thirst for a more authentic life, the impulse that led so many saints, from the ancient desert fathers to contemporary seekers, to rebel against the "deadness" of their surrounding culture and its false rewards. This leads to lessons on letting go, on work, on sitting still, and on learning to love—the final goal of all spiritual practice.

At this point the lessons grow harder. "Learning to Suffer" addresses the most difficult and yet the most necessary theme in any "guide to happiness," and here the wisdom of the saints is especially telling. For the saints do not show us how to avoid suffering, nor do they teach that suffering makes us happy. What they show is that it is only along the path of holiness that we can comprehend a type of happiness for which suffering is no necessary obstacle. The same applies to the subject of death. On the saint's path to happiness death is no longer an enemy or a fearsome end; learning to die, it appears, is an indispensable aspect of learning to live. Beyond this, there still remains a final lesson. For the saints do not regard death as the final chapter of the human story. Their vision is trained on a dimension of happiness even greater than this life can contain. Rather than undermine the importance of everyday life, this ultimate goal gives value and meaning to all that goes before.

The saints are those who embodied the deepest wisdom of Christianity. Naturally, their teaching has particular meaning for those who share their faith. Yet insofar as the saints have shared the human condition, their experience has a certain universal relevance. Much of this wisdom—on the value of detachment, good work, interior peace, and the importance of love—resonates with the practical advice of other counselors and guides. Among the most popular of recent inspirational maxims is "Don't sweat the small stuff." In a way this echoes the advice of Jesus to his disciple Martha of Bethany, when she complained that her sister Mary was not helping her in the kitchen: "Martha, Martha, you are anxious and troubled about many things; one thing is necessary."

Thomas Merton alluded to this story in words that relate

directly to the theme of this book: "Happiness consists in finding out precisely what the 'one thing necessary' may be, in our lives, and in gladly relinquishing all the rest. For then, by a divine paradox, we find that everything else is given us together with the one thing we needed."

What is the "one thing necessary"? Its form is different for each person, though its content is always the same. It is "to fulfill our own destiny, according to God's will, to be what God wants us to be."

✦

The "lessons" in this book are rooted not in my own wisdom or in any personal claim to holiness, but only in my own questions and my own search. It was that search that led me, many years ago, to drop out of college and make my way to the Catholic Worker, a "house of hospitality" on the Lower East Side of Manhattan. This radical Christian movement represents an ongoing effort to live out the gospel in community with the poor and in the service of peace. A number of motivations drew me there. At the age of nineteen, I was eager to experience something of life firsthand, not just from books. I was tired of living for myself alone and longed to give myself to something larger and more meaningful. I had a pretty good idea of what I was *against*; I wanted to find out what my life was *for*.

Dorothy Day, the movement's founder and the editor of its newspaper, was familiar with these motivations. "What's it all about—the Catholic Worker Movement?" she asked in one of her last columns. "It is, in a way, a school, a work camp, to which large-hearted, socially conscious young people come to find their vocations. After some months or years, they know most definitely what they want to do with their lives. Some go into medicine, nursing, law, teaching, farming, writing, and publishing. They learn not only to love, with compassion, but to overcome fear, that dangerous emotion that precipitates violence."

I remained at the Catholic Worker for five years—as it turned out, the last five years of Dorothy Day's life. By the time I left I had found much of what I had been seeking, and perhaps more. Among other things I had become a Catholic. The attraction of Catholicism had little to do with doctrine or the church's teaching authority, of which I comprehended very little. It had much more to do with the wisdom and example of its saints and the power of various spiritual classics. From St. Augustine I learned to see my life as part of God's own story of creation and grace. From Pascal I learned that the gospel message corresponds to the questions of my own heart. From Flannery O'Connor I learned what a difference it makes to see the world in the light of faith. And from Dorothy Day I learned to know and love the saints— not just as legendary figures from Christian history but as friends and contemporaries, as members of the family, which is how she talked about them.

It was Dorothy herself who first made me suspect that holiness and happiness were related. She was a person of extraordinary vitality—steeped in prayer, yet totally present to the person beside her. Keenly attuned to the suffering of others, she remained equally sensitive to signs of beauty and ever mindful of what she called "the duty of delight." She read the daily news in the light of eternity. And she had the remarkable effect, when you were with her, of making you feel that you could change the world, and be a better person, and that such an undertaking would be an enormous adventure.

In the years after I became a Catholic people often asked if I planned to become a priest or a monk. But ultimately, that was not my path. Instead I got married and had three children and went to work as an editor of religious books. And it is in that context, in the frequent bliss and the occasional bedlam of family life, that I have carried on my conversations with the saints. Sometimes their lives seem far removed from the world I live in. There are times when I fall into bed and think enviously of how easy it must be to find God in the quiet and solitude of a monastic cell!

But then the principal lesson of the saints occurs to me: the fact that for all of us it is our present situation and the given circumstances of our lives that provide our own road to holiness. This is my monastery! And if there is a way to God in my present life, I must learn to find it in the midst of work, of driving children to school, of walking the dog, of washing the dishes, and of responding to a hundred other demands on my time and attention. One learns to realize, for one thing, that it isn't necessary to flee to some special religious place to find occasions for the exercise of patience, humility, forgiveness, self-sacrifice, and generosity. A family can be an ideal place for this—better than a monastery in some respects. All this, even the writing of this book, is part of my way to God. That being so, it must be part of my own way to happiness.

✦

If there is one gospel text that recurs with regularity in the lives of the saints, it is the story of Jesus and the "rich young man" who came to him looking for the secret of happiness ("What must I do to inherit eternal life?"). Jesus told him,

"Go, sell all that you have and give to the poor, and come follow me." He was not calling this young man to a life of misery but to a new life, richer than anything he had known before. St. Mark notes significantly that Jesus looked on the man "and loved him." But evidently this was both too much and at the same time not enough for him. Perhaps he would have preferred a list of "five principles" or "ten easy steps." And so he went sadly away.

For so many of the saints this story represented the pivotal choice for their own lives. Would they respond to Jesus' challenge and invitation or would they too, like the young man in the story, walk sadly away? Happily, they chose the former. The lessons that follow describe some of what they saw and learned along the way.

THE
SAINTS' GUIDE
TO HAPPINESS

One

LEARNING TO BE ALIVE

We beg you, make us truly alive.　　—Serapion of Thmuis

Mine, O thou lord of life, send my roots rain.
　　　　　　　　　　　　　—Gerard Manley Hopkins

THE SORROWS OF LIFE are many. But sorrow is not the opposite of happiness. At least in sorrow we are aware of being alive. So often the problem is not really sorrow but the deadness that attends our daily existence. The pace and pressures of the world, the struggle to "make a living," the disquiet driven by constant advertising, the distracting drone of consumer culture—all these contribute to fatigue, numbness, an inability to feel anything at all. Our bodies may thrive—no generation has ever enjoyed such long life or good health—yet there is a sickness that eats away at our souls.

We can see it in the faces of commuters on a train or shoppers in the mall; too often it is in the face we encounter in the mirror. But we may also see it in the faces in church. Religion in itself offers no special immunity against deadness, especially when religious practice becomes simply another task to perform, a set of rules to obey. William Blake wrote scornfully of "priests in black gowns, walking their rounds, binding with briars my joys & desires."

Doubtless it often feels that way. But that is not the way it needs to be.

Of the flock in his care, Jesus said: "I came that they might have life and have it in abundance." Such life in abundance is one way of describing the meaning of happiness. It is an antidote to the kind of existence—dry and hollow—that dulls even the memory of our "joys & desires." Yet over the centuries too many Christians have transposed Christ's promise to the other side of death, thereby spurning the challenge to seek life and happiness in the present. Against this tendency St. Theophanis the Monk, one of the early desert fathers, warned, "Do not deceive yourself with idle hopes that in the world to come you will find life if you have not tried to find it in the present world."

St. Irenaeus, a second-century bishop and theologian, put it this way: "The glory of God is the human being fully alive." Irenaeus wrote these words to oppose a kind of spirituality that scorns material existence in the world. But his words pose a challenge for anyone who settles for a truncated life, whether reduced to work, entertainment, or an otherworldly spiritualism. To be fully alive—it was for this that we were created; it was toward this goal, as the saints remind us, that Christ pointed the way.

But we have lost our way.

What might it mean to be "fully alive"? Obviously it is not the same as simply eating and breathing. Nor is it expressed in a flurry of manic activity. To be fully alive is a matter of living out of the deepest part of oneself. Call it the heart or the soul; these are words that describe the central and intimate core of our being, the place where we are most truly ourselves. Given the noise and distractions that surround us, it is often hard to imagine that such places exist. We glide along the surface, taking our cues from the newspapers, or our neighbors, or the commercials on TV. They tell us what to desire, what to fear, and what will bring us joy. Yet the more we listen to such voices, the less we know ourselves. No wonder happiness is so elusive.

The men and women called saints have walked a different path, a path to God that was at the same time the path to their own true selves. There is much that they might teach us. Yet their authority as guides and teachers often fades in the shadow of an apparent "otherness" that renders them at once inaccessible and unappealing. To begin with, saints are supposed to be perfect people—"not like us." Traditional stories about their lives reinforce this impression, emphasizing miraculous and otherworldly traits while airbrushing anything recognizably human. On this basis we might share George Orwell's conclusion that the very aspiration to holiness is evidence of a warped personality. "Saints," he wrote, "should always be judged guilty until they are proved innocent."

Sentimental and saccharine hagiography is partly to blame. Dorothy Day wrote about coming across one book about saints that included this passage on their eating habits:

"The saints went to their meals sighing. St. Alphonsus, when sitting down, would think only of the sufferings of the souls in purgatory, and with tears would beseech Our Lady to accept the mortifications he imposed upon himself during meals. Blessed de Montfort sometimes shed tears and sobbed bitterly when sitting at table to eat." To this, Day offered the brief comment: "No wonder no one wants to be a saint."

Yet Day herself conveyed something else. No one who ever observed how she savored a cup of instant coffee or the rare luxury of a fresh roll, how she enjoyed watching the shifting tides of Raritan Bay off Staten Island or listened raptly to the Saturday afternoon opera broadcasts on the radio could fail to detect the quality that Teilhard de Chardin described as a "zest for living": "that spiritual disposition, at once intellectual and affective, in virtue of which life, the world, and action seem to us, on the whole, luminous— interesting—appetizing."

As the otherworldly heroes of pious legend, saints may seem close to God but not exactly human. In fact, as Thomas Merton observed, sanctity is really a matter of being more fully human: "This implies a greater capacity for concern, for suffering, for understanding, for sympathy, and also for humor, for joy, for appreciation for the good and beautiful things of life." One observes those qualities in holy persons of recent times—Mother Teresa, or Pope John XXIII, or the Dalai Lama—a certain lightness of being, far from the torturous attitude of Blessed de Montfort toward his food. And it makes one wonder if a similar quality or aura did not surround the great saints of the past—whether St. Francis of Assisi, who built the first Christmas crèche, or St. Teresa of Ávila, who prayed to God to "deliver us from sour-faced saints," or St. Francis de Sales, who said that a "sad saint is a sad sort of saint." They stood out not just for their faith or good works but for exhibiting a certain quality of being. In traditional Christian art this aura was represented by a halo. Real saints have no such distinguishing marks. But the aura is real. It is the presence of life, life in abundance.

✦

Far from that goal, mired in deadness, where does our road to happiness begin? It might begin with a certain restless disquiet, a sense of subtle dissatisfaction, the suspicion that "there must be *more* to life." Of course to this our culture has a ready answer: Indeed there is more, infinitely more— more things, more pleasures, more *fun*.

The world offers innumerable pleasures and distractions. But they cannot satisfy our deepest hunger. When we realize this, and if our disquiet remains intact, then we may find ourselves entering what Walker Percy, in *The Moviegoer*, calls the search: "The search is what anyone would undertake if he were not sunk in the everydayness of his own life. . . . To become aware of the possibility of the search is to be onto something. Not to be onto something is to be in despair."

The lineage of such searchers is long. It includes such a recent figure as Thomas Merton, self-described "complete twentieth-century man," who, at the dawn of World War II, abandoned the ambitions of his New York literary set to become a Trappist monk in rural Kentucky. Justifying this decision, he later wrote, "What I had abandoned when I 'left the world' and came to the monastery was the *understanding of myself* that I had developed in the context of civil so-

ciety—my identification with what appeared to me to be its
aims . . . the image of a society that is happy because it
drinks Coca-Cola or Seagram's or both and is protected by
the bomb."

The lineage reaches back to Henry David Thoreau, the
nineteenth-century sage of New England. In 1845 he withdrew to a hermitage on Walden Pond, near Concord, seeking
to escape a world in which "the mass of men lead lives of
quiet desperation." He decried the condition of everyday
life, which seemed to him no better than a kind of sleep-
walking. "To be awake is to be alive," he wrote. "I have not
yet met a man who was quite awake." And so he retreated
for a while to the New England equivalent of the desert,
hoping "to live deliberately, to front only the essential facts
of life and see if I could learn what it had to teach, and not,
when I came to die, discover that I had not lived."

It extends back considerably further . . .

TO THE DESERT

In the fourth century, just as Christianity had achieved a certain level of acceptance, there emerged a new phenomenon,
a source of wonder and fascination to Christians in late Roman society. Men and women—at first a few intrepid pio-
neers but gradually large numbers—began drifting into the
desert, their ranks gradually populating the seemingly un-
inhabitable corners of Palestine, Arabia, Syria, and Egypt.
Some gathered in small communities; others lived in remote
and isolated caves or among abandoned ruins. In their solitude they occupied themselves with prayer and fasting, reflection on scripture, and simple labor.

What did they seek? The possible answers are many: to live more deliberately, to seek a narrower road to salvation, to overcome the deadness they perceived in the surrounding culture, to tap into the source of life. Yes, all this. And yet it is striking how often the stories of these desert pilgrims relate their quest to the pursuit of happiness. There is St. Simeon Stylites (d. 459), who, after hearing a reading of the Beatitudes, prayed that God would lead him on the path of happiness and was led, curiously enough, to construct a series of pillars (or stylites), progressively higher from the ground, upon which he spent the next thirty-seven years of his life. There is the story of St. Macarius of Egypt, whose very name comes from the Greek word for happiness. While crossing the Nile one day, he overheard a soldier remark on his cheerful demeanor and declared, "You have reason to call us happy, for this is our name. But if we are happy in despising the world, are not you miserable who live slaves to it?"

The most famous of these desert fathers was St. Antony, who died in 356 at the remarkable age of 105. Born into a prosperous Christian family in Upper Egypt, Antony found his life radically transformed one Sunday when he heard the gospel story of Jesus and the rich young man. He was particularly struck by Christ's injunction "Go sell what you possess and give to the poor, and you will have treasure in heaven." Others in church that day presumably heard the same text, but Antony took it to heart. In short order he proceeded to shed all his property and to make his way to the wilderness, eventually settling in an abandoned hilltop fort in the Arabian Desert. There he lived for the next twenty years, spending his time in prayer, contemplation, and the upkeep of his small garden. When a visiting philosopher asked him how he could be so happy without "the consolation of books," Antony replied, "My book is the nature of created things, and anytime I want to read the words of God, the book lies open before me."

His story is recounted in a book by St. Athanasius (d. 373), the bishop of Alexandria. *The Life of Antony*, written shortly after the saint's death, spares no detail of Antony's various austerities and ordeals: hunger, thirst, and lack of sleep, not to mention the dangers of lions, crocodiles, snakes, and scorpions. The most dramatic episodes, however, involve Antony's assault by a succession of demons, which appeared to him under various forms and guises—both hideous and alluring—to tempt him from his path. Yet after all these ordeals, when Antony finally reemerged after his many years of solitude, everyone marveled at his physical fitness, for he was "neither fat from lack of exercise, nor emaciated from fasting and combat with demons."

His inner equilibrium was equally impressive: "His soul being free of confusion, he held his outer senses also undisturbed, so that from the soul's joy his face was cheerful as well, and from the movements of the body it was possible to sense and perceive the stable condition of the soul." Eventually he consented to serve as the abbot of a community of monks. According to Athanasius, who knew him, "He was never troubled, his soul being calm, and he never looked gloomy, his mind being joyous."

The desert monastics had a name for this kind of equilibrium. They called it *apatheia*—quite a different thing from the indifference or listlessness associated with "apathy." For the desert monastics true life began when one was no longer a prisoner of such feelings as anger, fear, lust, and pride. When all these passions were pruned away, the result was not an absence of feeling, but apatheia—a balance and wholeness expressed in kindness, gentleness, and compassion: the "soul's joy" so evident in the face of Antony or the "happiness" observable in St. Macarius.

The Life of Antony was a popular success. It spawned a whole literature of similar *vitae*, thus feeding an appetite in late antiquity for stories of spiritual heroism. Among those infected by the power of this story was St. Augustine, later the bishop of Hippo and one of the towering figures in Christian history. In his *Confessions* he recounted how, on the eve of his conversion, he received a visitor named Ponticianus, a Christian "who held a high position in the Emperor's household." From this gentleman he first heard the story of St. Antony and found himself "astonished to hear of the wonders [God] had worked so recently, almost in our own times." (Augustine was born in 354, two years before Antony's death.)

Augustine's astonishment, however, was joined by a certain anguish. Though for some time he had intellectually embraced the logic of Christianity, he had found it impossible to reconcile his life with his newfound convictions. Like the rich young man of the gospels, "I still postponed my renunciation of this world's joys, which would have left me free to look for that other happiness, the very search for which, let alone its discovery, I ought to have prized above the discovery of all human treasures and kingdoms. . . . All the time that Ponticianus was speaking my conscience gnawed away at me like this."

To Augustine, Antony's story described the search for happiness. Antony had found it; Augustine wanted it too.

From a distance of sixteen hundred years, it is hard to appreciate the appeal of such a story. Our society tends to idealize self-fulfillment, not self-denial. And so, in contrast with the happiness afforded by life among the scorpions, the miseries of our present "slavery" may seem fond and familiar.

Thomas Merton reflected this attitude when, on the eve of his own conversion, he came across a text by Aldous Huxley extolling the practice of asceticism: "Asceticism! The very thought of such a thing was a complete revolution in my mind. The word had so far stood for a kind of weird and ugly perversion of nature, the masochism of men who had gone crazy in a warped and unjust society. What an idea! To deny the desires of one's flesh, and even to practice certain disciplines that punished and mortified those desires: until this day, these things had never succeeded in giving me anything but gooseflesh."

Yet despite its negative associations, there was more to asceticism than mere self-punishment. The word comes from "ascesis," or training, such as that which an athlete might undertake. Anyone who has trained for a marathon knows what it means to endure physical deprivation for the sake of a goal. In similar fashion, the austerities and sacrifices of the desert monks were aimed at a discipline of the will, an intensity of focus and concentration on their spiritual goal. What was that goal? For the desert monks the flight from "the world" was really a rejection of "worldliness," a social agenda organized around the quest for power, property, pleasure, and status. If that sounds quaint, we might substitute for "the world" the values of Hollywood, Madison Avenue, Wall Street, or the Fox Network, the arbiters of a culture that favors image over reality, having over being.

The early monks sought a path from deadness to life. They fled "the world" not simply to spurn material pleasures, much less to punish themselves, but to "awaken" to a quality of existence deeper than custom, routine, and the bondage of social expectation. As Merton himself later came to appreciate, "What the [desert] Fathers sought most of all was their own true self in Christ. And in order to do that they had to reject completely the false, formal self, fabricated under social compulsion in 'the world.' They sought a way to God that was uncharted and freely chosen, not inherited from others who had mapped it out beforehand. They sought a God whom they alone could find, not one who was 'given' in a set stereotyped form by somebody else."

They were learning to be alive.

FREEDOM

Thomas Merton's eventual affinity for these spiritual explorers emerged from his own experience. In *The Seven Storey Mountain*, the autobiography he wrote early in his career as a Trappist monk, Merton described the journey that had led him from a life of aimless "captivity" in the world to the "freedom" of his enclosure within the four walls of a monastic cell. Even by monastic standards, the Trappists (the Order of Cistercians of the Strict Observance) enjoyed a reputation for extreme austerity, preserving, in dress, customs, and the spirit of silence, the character of their medieval roots. Merton, in contrast, appeared to be a complete product of the modern world. He had enjoyed a life of license, excitement, and the pursuit of pleasure only, in the end, to reject it all as an illusion. As he wrote, "If what most people take for granted were really true—if all you needed to be happy was to grab everything and see everything and investigate every experience and then talk about it, I should have been a very happy person, a spiritual millionaire, from the cradle even until now." He *should* have been a very happy person. But he was not.

The Seven Storey Mountain tells the tale—by turns funny and sad—of Merton's search for his true identity and home, beginning with his orphaned childhood and his education in France; in Cambridge, England (he was banished from the university on account of his scandalous behavior); and eventually at Columbia University in New York. There he perfected a pose of cool sophistication, smoking, drinking all night in jazz clubs, and writing novels in the style of James Joyce. He regarded himself as a true man of his age, free of any moral laws beyond his own making, ready to "ransack and rob" the world of all its pleasures and satisfactions. But increasingly his life struck him more as a story of pride and selfishness that brought nothing but unhappiness to himself and others. "What a strange thing!" he wrote. "In filling myself, I had emptied myself. In grasping things, I had lost everything. In devouring pleasures and joys, I had found distress and anguish and fear."

Out of his own anguish and confusion Merton found himself drawn by the sense that there must be a deeper end and purpose to existence. All around him the world was tumbling toward war, the ultimate achievement of "Contemporary Civilization." Meanwhile he was reading William Blake, St. Augustine, and medieval philosophy and beginning to suspect that "the only way to live was to live in a world that was charged with the presence and reality of God."

It was a short leap from this insight to his reception into the Catholic church and ultimately to the Abbey of Gethsemani. The Trappists had captured his heart from the first time he read about them in *The Catholic Encyclopedia*: "What wonderful happiness there was, then, in the world! There were still men on this miserably noisy, cruel earth, who tasted the marvelous joy of silence and solitude, who dwelt in forgotten mountain cells, in secluded monasteries, where the news and desires and appetites and conflicts of the world no longer reached them." When he later made a retreat at Gethsemani and there for the first time viewed the silent monks, dressed in their white habits and kneeling in prayer in the chapel, he felt that he had found his true home at last. "This is the center of America," he exclaimed.

In his own lifetime Thomas Merton became a hugely popular spiritual writer. In the decades since his death in 1968 that popularity has remained steady. Relatively few among his readers may have followed his route to the monastery. Yet countless others have identified with his experience. They have felt the insufficiency of "what most people take for granted" in the pursuit of happiness. They have heard the call to fullness of life, a call beyond the agenda of a world out of kilter. And they have reacted as St. Augustine did to the story of St. Antony: with astonishment "to hear of the wonders God had worked so recently, almost in our own times."

One of these readers was James Martin, a young American Jesuit priest, whose memoir, *In Good Company*, describes his own "fast track" from the corporate world to a life rooted in traditional monastic vows of poverty, chastity, and obedience. Although he was raised as a nominal Catholic, Martin's youthful ambitions were unaffected by any religious concerns. His studies fueled by dreams of "high-powered jobs" and "mountains of money," he enrolled in the prestigious Wharton School of Business. By the time he was in his mid-twenties he was well on his way—a junior executive at General Electric, rapidly climbing the corporate ladder. Yet before long he found himself at a point of complete confusion and unhappiness. "Simply put, I couldn't figure out the *point* of what I was doing with my life. Something basic was missing. . . . Is this life?"

Martin's disquiet was enhanced by the cold and impersonal atmosphere of the corporate workplace, the callous "downsizing," the constant pressure to make the quarterly "numbers." Increasingly he was struck by the feeling that his life had "no real order, no real purpose, and no real meaning." At mass one Sunday he heard the same gospel story that had once struck St. Antony: Jesus' invitation to the rich young man to sell all that he had and "come, follow me." Inevitably Martin identified with the young man in the story. "That was me," he reflected, "a rich, young (and depressed) man."

A turning point came one day when he happened to see a documentary on public television about the life of Thomas Merton. He had never heard of Merton. Yet something in this story, some sense of a greater reality, a more abundant life, captured his imagination. The next day he went out and picked up a copy of *The Seven Storey Mountain*. What he read corresponded powerfully with his own experience. "Thomas Merton seemed to have struggled with the same problems I did: vanity, false ambition, careerism. The more he confessed his shortcomings, the more I felt the urge to listen to what he had to say, and the more resonance I felt within me."

A strange impulse, at first mysterious, but increasingly irresistible, began sounding within him: the thought that he would like to become a priest. He tried pushing this thought away. But underneath there was a growing certainty: "I wanted to live the kind of life that Thomas Merton lived— even though I didn't much understand it. I wanted to feel the calm that he felt when he entered the monastery."

In the end he found that calm, not by living the life that Merton lived, or St. Augustine, or St. Antony, but in his own way, as a Jesuit, living in a world that was "charged with the presence and reality of God."

MORNING STAR

The happiness of the saints does not consist of adding up mortifications and self-conscious exercises. It does not require that we ascend a pillar or stand in freezing water with arms outstretched, as the ancient Celtic monks liked to do. What surprises and attracts us in the best of the saints is not the heaviness of their burdens but the "soul's joy" that shines through their actions and attitudes. It is not their ponderousness that appeals to us but their levity.

Among the sayings of the desert fathers there is this exchange between a younger monk and one of his elders: "Abbot Lot came to Abbot Joseph and said: 'Father: according as I am able, I keep my little rule, and my little fast, my prayer, meditation, and contemplative silence; and according as I am able to strive to cleanse my heart of thoughts: now what more should I do?' The elder rose up in reply and stretched out his hands to heaven, and his fingers became like ten lamps of fire. He said: 'Why not be totally changed into fire?' "

The austerity of a desert hermit or the discipline of a

Trappist monk is not for everyone. But if these paths are not for us, there still remains the challenge to resist the downward drift of the world, to take possession of our own souls, to incline our hearts to the source of life, and to know, before we die, that we have truly lived. If we succeed, we may become, like the saints, a source of life and light to others. As St. Antony liked to say, "The Fathers of old went forth into the desert, and when themselves were made whole, they became physicians, and returning again they made others whole."

✦

Thoreau too, after venturing forth into the relative wilderness of Walden Pond, eventually returned to Concord. Apparently, the experience of two years of solitude had better equipped him to continue his explorations in the midst of society. "I left the woods for as good a reason as I went there," he explained. "Perhaps it seemed to me that I had several more lives to live, and could not spare any more time for that one."

Thoreau was keenly sensitive to the seductive encroachments of routine and convention and their capacity to make sleepwalkers of us all: "It is remarkable how easily and insensibly we fall into a particular route, and make a beaten track for ourselves. . . . The surface of the earth is soft and impressible by the feet of men; and so with the paths which the mind travels. How worn and dusty, then, must be the highways of the world, how deep the ruts of tradition and conformity!"

But deadness does not have the last word in his story. Thoreau's reflections in *Walden* conclude with a remarkable image, that of a "strong and beautiful bug which came out of the dry leaf of an old table of apple-tree wood, which had stood in a farmer's kitchen for sixty years," a bug hatched from an egg deposited many years earlier in the living tree from which the table was fashioned. "Who," he asked, "does not feel his faith in a resurrection and immortality strengthened by hearing of this? Who knows what beautiful and winged life, whose egg has been buried for ages under many concentric layers of woodenness in the dead dry life of society, deposited at first in the alburnum of the green and living tree, which has been gradually converted into the semblance of its well-seasoned tomb . . . may unexpectedly come forth from amidst society's most trivial and handselled furniture, to enjoy its perfect summer life at last!"

That "beautiful bug" is a fitting symbol for the spirit of life submerged beneath the encrustations of our everyday existence, that capacity that lies within us, even when all seems cold and numb, like a tulip bulb in winter—not dead, after all, but merely sleeping.

Thoreau's words resonate with the ancient challenge to wake up, to shake off the coils of slumber, to learn how to be more fully alive. "Only that day dawns to which we are awake," he wrote. "There is more day to dawn. The sun is but a morning star."

Two

LEARNING TO LET GO

If you look carefully you will see that there is one thing and only one thing that causes unhappiness. The name of that thing is Attachment. What is an attachment? An emotional state of clinging caused by the belief that without some particular thing or some person you cannot be happy.

—Anthony de Mello

"HOW HAPPY are the poor in spirit, for theirs is the kingdom of heaven." With these words Jesus introduced the Beatitudes—a preamble to the Sermon on the Mount and a distillation of his essential teachings. Generations past counting have pondered this "beatitude," wondering to what degree the happiness of spiritual poverty obliges one to be actually poor—or perhaps more to the point, to what degree Jesus' intentions can be reconciled with the pursuit of private property. But whatever Jesus had in mind, this much is clear: It is difficult to reconcile his intentions with the spirit of the modern shopping mall.

Our society surrounds us with a great cloud of enticement. Wherever we turn we confront the claim that happiness is just around the corner, a matter of having more or better or newer things. The fathers of American capitalism certainly endorsed this creed. John D. Rockefeller, when asked what would make him happy, is said to have replied, "One dollar more."

Our economy relies on such unstinting desire. In the sad aftermath of September 11, when many Americans, stunned with grief, seemed to lose their taste for spending, President Bush personally urged the public to get up and go shopping. But special prompting is not ordinarily necessary. We need only peruse the pages of any popular magazine. Each advertisement is a window on a parallel universe, where beautiful and apparently happy people invite us to share the pleasures that expensive cars, new clothes, and shiny hair can provide. The siren call of these voices is so ubiquitous that we hear them in our dreams.

But it is not only property that we grasp and hold. We may cling to many things: our security, our self-image, the sense of being "in control," the overpowering conviction of *being right*. We prize respectability, the desire to be thought better than we really are. We even cling to our miseries. How difficult it is to let go of an injury, a shameful memory, or anxieties about the future. What would it mean to let go of all this? Where does the happiness of the Beatitudes begin?

It might begin with an act of forgiveness, a decision to erase the mental tally of ancient wrongs and unpaid debts. It might involve the tranquil acceptance of circumstances beyond our control or the recognition that not everything has to be perfect. Insofar as we define ourselves by what we lack, letting go might begin with an expression of gratitude, some gracious acknowledgement of all we do have and how much we owe to others. Ideally, what is left after we have let go of our attachments is a kind of poverty. Call it what you will—

emptiness, freedom, simplicity; according to the saints, there lies the way to happiness.

THE HOOK OF ATTACHMENT

The acquisitive spirit is not a recent phenomenon. The desert fathers and mothers identified it as a demonic spirit—"a demon of sadness," as Evagrius Ponticus put it—who "lays his snares and produces sadness precisely where he sees we are particularly inclined." It was in part to escape this demon that so many of them went to the desert in the first place. Their solution was not simply to discard excess property. They were aware that mere external stripping was useless without a deeper inner conversion. According to a monk known as Abba Moses, there are those "who have given away worldly wealth in gold or silver or lands, and who are afterwards agitated about a knife, a pencil, a pin, or a pen. . . . They have given up all their property for the love of Christ; and yet keep their old acquisitive attitude over little things and quickly become upset over them." He scoffed at St. Peter, the onetime fisherman, and his boast to the Lord: "Lo, we have left all and followed thee. What shall we have therefore?" As Abba Moses noted, "It is clear that they had left nothing but their miserable broken nets."

In ridding themselves of possessions, the desert monastics sought to remove the hook of attachment from their own hearts. Poverty was not embraced for its own sake. It was just another "tool of the trade"—as such, no more than a means toward their ultimate goal, "purity of heart." Through ascetical disciplines like fasting, prayer, and poverty, they sought to uproot all the "brambles and weeds" (anger, lust, greed, and envy, for example) that choked their hearts and smothered their capacity to love. Some of them took this to extremes. A monk named Serapion sold his book of the gospels and distributed the proceeds to the poor, remarking, "I have sold the book which told me to sell all that I had and give to the poor."

But if the practice of monastic poverty took its cue from the gospels, it also reflected certain practical insights into human nature. Among these was the recognition that as long as our happiness is tied to "one dollar more" our goal inevitably eludes us. As St. Antony observed, "Those who are not satisfied with what they have to sustain life, but who seek for more, make themselves slaves of passions which trouble the soul and introduce into it ever worse thoughts and fantasies—that everything is bad and, therefore, that new and better things must be acquired."

The peril of this passion for "new and better things" is the moral of dozens of children's tales. Among these is the fable of the foolish fisherman and his wife who, as a reward for sparing the life of a magical fish, are granted their heart's desire. What should they wish for? They begin with modest improvements in their circumstances: a larger house, a pretty garden. But their desires quickly escalate, assuming ever more extravagant forms. The house gives way to a mansion and then a palace. Ultimately nothing satisfies them. They reach too far, the bubble bursts, and they are restored once again to their humble origins. The key to happiness, we may infer, is not to have all that you desire but instead to desire (or better, to be satisfied with) what you have.

Such satisfaction entails a certain letting go—not so much of things as of the illusion that happiness depends on attaining what we currently lack. Though many of the saints embraced actual poverty, they did more than simply spurn worldly goods. They lived out of a different center of value—as Jesus put it, laying up treasure where neither moth nor rust could consume. Having accomplished this, they found that other things—wealth and property, certainly, but also false ambitions, anxieties, and petty resentments— tended to fall away of their own weight.

"Consider the lilies," said Jesus, "how they grow; they neither toil nor spin, yet I tell you, even Solomon in all his glory was not arrayed like one of these" (Matt. 6:28–29). The gospels are filled with similar exhortations to trust and radical simplicity. There may be a limit to what we can learn from a lily. But we are not bereft of other models.

THE POOR MAN

Among all the saints of history St. Francis of Assisi (1182–1226) enjoys a special status. As the saint whose life most closely calls to mind the example of Christ, he is one of the few widely honored beyond the boundaries of the church. But he is also, significantly, the one whose joyfulness was a defining mark of his holiness. Whether in taming the ferocious wolf of Gubbio, or preaching to a flock of sparrows, or in his canticle to "Brother Sun and Sister Moon," Francis's writings and the stories that adorn his legend draw a consistent portrait of his happy disposition, his celebration of the goodness of God, and his delight in the beauty of creation. It is clear, however, that his capacity for joy in God's service was directly related to his progress in the way of detachment. Francis was, above all, a master of the art of letting go.

His life began otherwise. As the son of a wealthy cloth merchant of Assisi, Francis was one of the privileged young men of his town. Attracted to adventure, frivolity, and romance, he passed his time among his friends, carousing and writing songs. When he was about twenty, a war broke out between Assisi and Perugia, a neighboring city-state. Francis eagerly took up arms and rode off, dreaming of glory, to join the fight. But the face of war—up close—was far from glorious. After surviving the carnage, and several additional months as a prisoner of war, he returned home, sick and broken. In the place of his previous gaiety he felt only a desperate emptiness, a feeling that there must be more to life than the success his parents envisioned for him. He took to wandering the outskirts of town, where for the first time he noticed the poor and the sick and the squalor in which they lived. What he saw repulsed him.

Francis had always been a fastidious person, keenly alert to beauty and appalled by ugliness. But then one day, as he was out riding, he came upon a leper by the side of the road. The poor man's face was horribly deformed, and he stank of disease. Nevertheless, Francis dismounted and, still careful to remain at arm's length, offered him a few coins. Then, moved by some impulse, he bent down and kissed the leper's ravaged hands. It was a turning point. From that encounter Francis's life began to take shape around an utterly new agenda, contrary to the values of his family and his society. In kissing the leper, he was not only dispensing with his fear of death and disease but letting go of a whole identity based on status, security, and worldly success.

Over the following weeks Francis became increasingly profligate in his charity, so much so that his father accused him of stealing from his warehouse to distribute to the poor.

Feeling desperate, he had Francis arrested and dragged before the bishop in the public square. Francis apologized for giving what was not his own. But he went further. In another extravagant gesture he stripped off his rich garments and handed them over to his astonished father. Standing naked before the crowd, Francis proclaimed: "Hitherto I have called you father on earth; but now I say 'Our Father, who art in heaven.' " The bishop hastened to cover him with a peasant's frock, but the transformation was accomplished. Francis had become the *Poverello*, the little poor man.

At first this spectacle attracted only ridicule. But gradually Francis exerted a subversive appeal. One by one he was joined by other young men of Assisi. Renouncing their property and their family ties, they flocked to Francis, becoming before long the nucleus of a new religious order, the Friars Minor. In time, beginning with the arrival of Clare, the daughter of another wealthy family of Assisi, they were joined by a company of female counterparts.

Francis and his companions lived outdoors or in primitive shelters. They worked alongside peasants in the fields in exchange for their daily bread. When there was no work, they begged or went hungry. Otherwise they tended the sick, comforted the sorrowful, and preached the gospel to those who would listen, an audience, in the case of Francis, that extended to flocks of birds as well as other creatures.

What was his appeal? Even his follower Brother Masseo asked this question, only half in jest: "Why you? Why does all the world seem to be running after you, and everyone seems to want to see you and hear you and obey you? You are not a handsome man. You do not not have great learning or wisdom. You are not a nobleman. So why is all the world running after you?"

Francis, with characteristic humility, explained that God's glory shone all the brighter for the weakness of such an obviously "miserable servant." Nevertheless, at least part of the answer had to do with his evident authenticity. Those who encountered Francis could no longer maintain that Christ's teachings were wonderful in theory but impossible to put into practice. Even the worldly Pope Innocent III felt compelled to endorse the new order. As one of his cardinals observed, "This man merely wishes us to live according to the Gospel. Now if we tell him that this surpasses human strength, then we are declaring that it is impossible to follow the Gospel, and blaspheming Christ, the author of the Gospel."

There was more. The example of Francis was not simply edifying but also deeply appealing. He exuded a spirit of freedom and joy. People *wanted* to be near him, to discover for themselves the secret of his joy. As Thomas of Celano, his first biographer, described him, "O how beautiful, how splendid, how glorious did he appear in the innocence of his life, in the simplicity of his words, in the purity of his heart, his love for God, in his fraternal charity, in his ardent obedience, in his peaceful submission, in his angelic countenance!" Here was a man who had evidently discovered the way to heaven. Others were eager to follow.

No doubt Francis's espousal of poverty was extreme. His was not the well-ordered simplicity of a monastery or the romantic poverty of the bohemian. It was the precarious and vulnerable poverty of the truly poor. Even sympathetic observers questioned so radical a stance. "One day the bishop of Assisi said to St. Francis: 'Your way of life without possessions of any kind seems to me very harsh and difficult.' 'My Lord,' Francis answered, 'if we had possessions we should need arms for their defense. They are the source of quarrels and lawsuits, and are usually a great obstacle to the love of God and one's neighbor. That is why we have no desire for temporal goods.' "

Francis turned worldly values upside down. Where others saw security, he saw only captivity; what for others represented success was for him a source of strife, an "obstacle to the love of God and one's neighbor." Moreover, for Francis, letting go did not end with wealth or property. He also let go of his reputation and status in society, his fastidiousness, his anger, his pride, and his ambitions—everything, in short, that hindered his ability to love. In the end he was not left barren. Rather the space in his heart previously occupied by all these things was now filled with a joy greater than anything the world could provide. His gratefulness exceeded his powers of description. Addressing his Creator, he wrote: "You are love, charity; You are wisdom, You are humility, You are patience. You are beauty, You are meekness, You are security, You are inner peace. You are joy, You are our hope and joy. . . . Great and wonderful Lord, All-powerful God, Merciful Savior."

Nearly eight hundred years later the example of St. Francis continues to exert a powerful appeal. As Carlo Carretto, a modern admirer, observed, "At least once in our lives we have dreamed of becoming saints. . . . Stumbling under the weight of the contradictions of our lives, for a fleeting moment we glimpsed the possibility of building within ourselves a place of simplicity and light. . . . This is when St. Francis entered our lives in some way."

Inspired by his example, we may dream of doing great things, performing heroic deeds, resolving all the contradictions of our lives with one kiss of a leper. But as Dorothy

Day wrote, "Sometimes it takes [just] one step. We would like to think so. And yet the older I get, the more I see that life is made up of many steps, and they are very small affairs, not giant strides. I have 'kissed a leper,' not once but twice—consciously—and I cannot say I am much the better for it."

Francis's style of radical detachment may be for only a few. But whether it is by small steps or in one giant stride, the value of letting go is not simply that it is better to be empty-handed. Rather the point is that the alternative—clinging to whatever we can get our hands on—incapacitates us for any greater prize. Until we have learned the art of letting go, the world presents us with innumerable snares and obstacles to our happiness. The challenge is not to renounce the world as such, but to let go of that grasping part of us that renders the world opaque. When that is accomplished, as Thomas à Kempis noted in *The Imitation of Christ*, then "every created thing will become for you a mirror of life and a book of holy teaching. For there is nothing created so small and mean that it does not reflect the goodness of God."

RESTLESS HEARTS

The question remains: If attachments and desires make us anxious and out of sorts, why then do we cling to them? Many have pondered this question, though none more deeply than St. Augustine of Hippo. As one of the great architects of Christian thought, Augustine left his mark on virtually every aspect of doctrine. But to the complex interplay between the self, the things of this world, and the pursuit of happiness, he devoted some of his most personal and poignant reflections. Augustine believed that the yearning for happiness is one of the defining characteristics of the human person: "Everyone, whatever his condition, desires to be happy. There is no one who does not desire this, and each one desires it with such earnestness that it is preferred to all other things; whoever, in fact, desires other things, desires them for this end alone. . . ."

According to Augustine, everything we do—even what is wrong or harmful—has happiness as its object. But we are misguided about how to obtain it; we seek from created things more than they can supply. The result is sadness, frustration, and anxiety. As he put it to God, "You made us for yourself and our hearts are restless until they rest in you."

His reflections on this subject emerged from his own experience, a story recounted in the *Confessions*. In this autobiographical work Augustine presented himself, the future bishop of Hippo, as a youth of exceptional promise yet a prisoner of his own unruly passions. His brilliance and ambition led him to a career as a professor of rhetoric, first in Carthage and later in Milan, at the time the seat of the Roman Empire. At the same time his quest for the meaning of life led him to explore the various philosophical and religious movements of his day. But none of them, he found, could adequately resolve his questions, least of all the mysteries of his own heart.

Augustine identified the major problem of his life as the contradiction between his longing for happiness and a sense of helpless bondage to compulsive desires and feelings that brought suffering to himself and those around him. Though he alluded frequently to the "brambles of lust," the problem ran deeper than unregulated sexuality. In one famous episode, treated at considerable length, he analyzed his role in a boyhood raid on a neighbor's pear tree, a bit of mischief inspired not by hunger or need but by sheer willfulness. It is a story that deliberately calls to mind the disobedience of Adam and Eve in the Garden of Eden. For Augustine it served the same function, as the paradigmatic expression of human sin. He termed it concupiscence, a debilitating, grasping desire that holds our will as its prisoner.

The signs of this concupiscence were visible to Augustine in every corner of his life, from the selfishness of his infancy and his later theft from his parents' larder to the first stirrings of adolescent lust and his desperate search for some "object for my love." These were not pleasant experiences; they brought only "pain, confusion, and error."

Augustine was largely responsible for defining the doctrine of original sin, an idea of greater subtlety than is usually supposed. He understood the expression of this sin as a disorder of the affections—not that we love too much but that we love *inordinately*; we fail to love things according to their true value. This, according to Augustine, is the basic condition of fallen humanity. It is not simply "lust" that leads us astray. Imagining ourselves the center of our own little universe, we are misguided even in our desire for good things—for love, for beauty, for truth. Our selfishness turns hunger to gluttony, love to lust, attraction to greedy possessiveness.

These insights emerged from his own painful journey. After years of searching, and the tearful prayers of his mother, Monica, he had come to the point of accepting the claims of Christianity. The scriptural account of creation and the fall, he had concluded, made sense of his own experience, explaining not only his restless unhappiness and the anxiety that soured his pleasures but also his growing apprehension of a truth and beauty beneath the surface of this world. Yet he continued to hold back, his will still bound, if only by a thread. "Give me chastity and continence," he prayed, "but not yet."

Augustine's tension reached a crisis as he walked one day in a garden. In the *Confessions* he presented this episode as a call to surrender, a kind of letting go. It was *attachments* that bound him—not to persons or things but to his own sins: "I was held back by mere trifles, the most paltry inanities, all my old attachments. They plucked at my garment of flesh and whispered, 'Are you going to dismiss us? From this moment we shall never be with you again, forever and ever.'"

As he wrestled with this conflict, he heard what seemed to be the voice of a child, saying, "Take and read." A Bible lay at hand. Opening it at random, he found the Pauline text "Not in reveling and drunkenness, not in lust and wantonness, not in quarrels and rivalries. Rather, arm yourselves with the Lord Jesus Christ; spend no more thought on nature and nature's appetites." In coming to the end of that sentence, he suddenly felt as if "the light of confidence flooded into my heart, and all the darkness of doubt was dispelled."

Augustine's breakthrough did not entail renouncing property, other people, or even "the world." It was his old self, the ravening maw of his own ego, that he had to let go. Only in this way could he see and love the beautiful things of this world—not simply as objects to possess, control, or consume but in terms of their true value. In loving God above all else, he was released from the coil of his *inordinate* affections. The world was no longer a snare. Instead all creation echoed his hymn of praise and thanksgiving: "Happiness is to rejoice in You and for You and because of You. This is true happiness and there is no other."

AN EXCHANGE OF GIFTS

We needn't go to the wilderness to begin resisting the seductive allure of an acquisitive culture. Nor do we need to strip ourselves like St. Francis to find some measure of his freedom. But if we would understand the happiness of the saints, we must learn how to move by steady degrees from a sense of ourselves based on what we have or what we lack and toward an understanding of who we really are. In this movement the challenge of letting go refers to more than our material attachments or even our evident faults and sins. The world is filled with unhappy people, burdened by regrets, the memory of past injuries, and the weight of all the sorrows and unfairness of their lives. Over time we can become so accustomed to these burdens that we cannot imagine what it would feel like to lay them down. And so, like the "rich young man" in the gospels, we "walk sadly away," preferring even hollow treasures to an unfamiliar alternative.

The saints chose another way: to let go, to follow with empty hands.

Among these saints was Catherine of Genoa, a beautiful Italian noblewoman of the fifteenth century. Her one desire from childhood was to enter a religious order. But her parents had different ideas. When she was fifteen, they arranged her marriage to the son of a rival family. Evidently the match was intended to achieve a reconciliation between the two long-feuding families, a case of Romeo and Juliet in reverse. Unfortunately, in this case, the matchmakers had given little weight to the incompatibility between Catherine and her husband. While she was modest and devout, her husband, in the words of her biographer, "was entirely the opposite in his mode of life." In the face of his compulsive gambling and flagrant infidelities, Catherine quickly sank into a state of depression that lasted for the first five years of her marriage.

For another five years Catherine tried to dispel her unhappiness by throwing herself into the frivolous diversions of high society. But this only left her feeling sadder and emptier. Finally, at the age of twenty-five, she uttered a desperate prayer for some relief from the torment of her existence, even praying for an illness that would confine her to bed.

Instead, one day in 1473, while kneeling for confession, she was suddenly overcome with remorse for the mediocrity of her life and at the same time with an overwhelming sense of God's goodness and mercy. "No more world," she was heard to utter. "No more sins." She resolved to let go of all the carefully hoarded resentments that had cramped her spirit. From that moment, by all accounts, she began to live a new life.

The first thing Catherine did was to go to work at the local hospital, hardly ordinary behavior for a woman of her social standing. She began with washing patients and cleaning their bedpans. No job was too repugnant. The miracle, though, was that as she grew in the practice of love, living no longer for herself alone, she also found herself growing in her capacity for happiness.

Around this time, as it happened, her husband's freespending ways finally reduced the couple to bankruptcy. No matter, they gave up their grand house and moved into a simple cottage, much more to Catherine's taste. Eventually, in part through her example, her husband reformed his own life, even becoming a lay Franciscan. They moved into an apartment in the hospital, where, after many years of work, Catherine assumed the job of director.

Catherine remained a laywoman throughout her life, even after her husband's death. Still, she attracted a wide circle of spiritual followers, drawn not only by the opportunity to work alongside her but also by the chance to benefit from her wisdom. In her final years she wrote several spiritual treatises and often experienced mystical ecstasies; it was said that she conversed with angels. Yet this profound "otherworldliness" was combined with scrupulous attention to practical detail, as well as constant availability to the needs of others.

St. Catherine's story parallels the lives of many other saints. They show us that the task of letting go—whether it applies to our things, our past, our sadness, or whatever else we cling to—is not simply a matter of giving something up. It is more in the nature of a swap. One identity or condition of life is exchanged for another, oriented now on a different goal, animated by a different spirit. Letting go is not a form of tightfisted austerity, the spiritual equivalent of a crash diet. On the contrary, it is a matter of relaxing our grip. By the same token, spiritual poverty does not translate into any arbitrary standard of living. Ultimately it refers to where our treasure lies. And where our treasure lies, as Jesus noted, there will our hearts be also.

Three

LEARNING TO WORK

There can be no joy in living without joy in work.
—St. Thomas Aquinas

IN THEIR CAVES in the desert, far from any employer or taskmaster, the early monks devoted a good part of every day to manual labor—gardening, basketmaking, or weaving. Thus they provided for their material needs, heeding St. Paul's fierce injunction, "If anyone will not work, let him not eat" (2 Thess. 3:10). Far from regarding such work as a distraction from their spiritual goal, they embraced it as a blessing, a kind of occupational therapy, to ward off boredom and sadness.

From the legends of the desert fathers it is clear that such work had a value in itself, quite apart from any wider utility or reward. A typical story concerns one Abba Paul, who, like his fellow hermits, spent much of his time weaving baskets of palm fronds. When the baskets filled his cave to capacity, he would set fire to them all and start again.

Such a tale might well illustrate the definition of folly. But for the monk's early chronicler it had a different meaning. Thus Abba Paul "proved that without working with his hands a monk cannot endure to abide in his place, nor can he climb any nearer the summit of holiness."

So much of our own work—in the light of eternity— reflects a similar folly. We sweep the floor that will be dusty again tomorrow. We write books that will go out of print and turn to dust on someone else's floor. Yet work is an inescapable part of the human condition. It is not simply the way we occupy a significant portion of our day; it is more than merely a way to pay our bills. It also represents in some sense our distinctively human place in the universe. Through work we participate in the unfolding of creation; in confronting materials and solving problems, we form our own character as well.

Whether accomplished in solitude or to public acclaim, work that is performed with fullness of heart is a gift that can only be given freely. It may employ principally our bodies or our minds, but it can always employ our souls. For that reason, it is hard to imagine how any credible prescription for happiness could ignore the importance of work.

Yet so often popular "advertisements" for happiness do exactly that. With our working hours carefully bracketed, we are urged to reserve the imagination of happiness for vacation or "leisure time." Work is simply an onerous necessity, a means of "earning a living," while happiness comes with the freedom from necessity, a neverland of golf and parties and holiday cruises. But the pleasures of idleness, like a constant diet of cake and ice cream, wear thin. There is a deeper happiness in a task, a project, a work that engages our hearts and endows our existence with purpose and meaning. In the right spirit, as the saints have shown, it is possible to find that meaning or happiness in virtually any task.

WORK AND HOLINESS

Leo Tolstoy explored this theme in one of the "moral tales" from his later years. In "A Talk Among Leisured People," he depicts a group of guests at a country estate, whose conversation one evening takes a serious turn: "They spoke of people present and absent, but failed to find anyone who was satisfied with his life. Not only could no one boast of happiness, but not a single person considered that he was living as a Christian should do. All confessed that they were living worldly lives concerned only for themselves and their families, none of them thinking of their neighbors, still less of God."

In this tale Tolstoy rehearsed his own struggles, particularly the tension he felt between the burdens of social expectation and his spiritual yearnings. By middle age the celebrated author of *War and Peace* and *Anna Karenina* had arrived at a point of near-suicidal despair. After a life of privilege and ease, guaranteed by his aristocratic upbringing and his literary success, he had found himself at a dead end. What was the point of it all?

His reflections led him to conclude that the pursuit of happiness is inseparable from the call to holiness, the effort to conform one's life to the rule of God, summarized, as he believed, in the Sermon on the Mount. But the pattern of such holiness, for Tolstoy, could not be found in any church or monastery so much as in the common life of the working poor. He derived this insight by comparing the members of his own privileged class with the peasants on his estate. Whatever their hardships, he concluded, these plain folk managed to rise in the morning, work a full day, and retire in the evening with a basic confidence in the goodness of life. Doubtless this conception of peasant life was somewhat romanticized. But his knowledge of "leisured people" came from personal experience. By emulating the peasants and their life of simplicity, faith, and work, Tolstoy hoped to find the happiness that had eluded him.

In "A Talk Among Leisured People" one of the dinner guests articulates this very resolution. He is an idealistic young man who asks his grumbling companions why they all must complain about their unhappy lives. Why not simply live as God instructs us? He himself will begin immediately: "I will renounce my property and go to the country and live among the poor," he declares. "I will work with them, will learn to labor with my hands, and if my education is of any use to the poor I will share it with them, not through institutions and books but directly by living with them in a brotherly way."

This was the ideal that Tolstoy set for himself. Turning over the royalties from his great novels to his family, he set out to live a simple life on his estate, Yasnaya Polyana. He even took to working in the fields alongside the peasants. The greatest error of the "leisure class," he proclaimed, was the erroneous belief that "felicity consists in idleness." We must return to the recognition "that work, and not idleness, is the indispensable condition of happiness for every human being."

But it was not so simple. Tolstoy could never fully embrace the ideals he preached. He quarreled incessantly with his family. He worked in the fields when it suited him, then went home to sleep on silk sheets. His quest for happiness was marked by the ambivalence and divided conscience that accompanied him until his death, at the age of eighty-two, in a railway stationmaster's house in Astapovo, the tiny village where he collapsed during a final flight from his home and family. The same tensions were prefigured in his story when the young dinner guest's idealistic resolution elicits only protest and scorn. One by one the rest of the guests try to point out the folly and irresponsibility of his intended path. Finally, it is left to one of their number, hitherto silent, to remark on the irony of the proceedings: "We all say that it would be good to live as God bids us but . . . it seems that none of us may live rightly: we may only talk about it."

To live rightly . . . Many would agree that this is the basis of happiness. But what constitutes right living? In the sense that Tolstoy envisioned, it is more than simply submitting to an external moral code. It means being on track, a condition in which our happiness and the striving for holiness converge. Such a condition is possible if the moral code of the universe is somehow actually inscribed on our souls. Such a life defies the common wisdom of the world—at least that wisdom bred from fantasies of winning the lottery ("Win a million dollars, quit your job, sleep 'til noon!"). According to Tolstoy, it describes a vision of everyday life, though lived under the dispensation of love and solidarity, rather than selfishness and competition. Does it matter that Tolstoy himself never achieved the balance he prescribed? For his view of the right relation among work, happiness, and holiness, he would certainly find wide support in the lives of the saints.

It was not for saints to discover the necessity of work. In the Book of Genesis, after all, God confronts Adam with the fruit of his disobedience: "In the sweat of your face you shall eat bread till you return to the ground." On this basis some Christians have regarded work as a curse, a proof of our fallen nature. But for most saints, the challenge has been to reconcile necessity and happiness, to find a way that work and everyday tasks can be blessed and ordered to a holy life. As Meister Eckhart, a fourteenth-century German mystic, put it, "To be right, a person must do one of two things: either he must learn to have God in his work and hold fast to Him there, or he must give up his work altogether. Since, however, we cannot live without activities that are both human and various, we must learn to keep God in everything we do."

"To keep God in everything we do," to find a balance between work and prayer—these were essential features of monastic life going back to the Rule of St. Benedict, the foundation for the Western monastic tradition. St. Benedict, an Italian abbot who died in 550, directed in his rule that each day should be carefully divided among prayer, study, and work, whether copying manuscripts, tending to the kitchen, or laboring in the fields. None of these tasks was more important or highly esteemed than another. According to Benedict, the monk should not be vexed when he must work in the fields, "For they are truly monks when they must live by manual labor, as did our fathers and the apostles."

St. Benedict's attitude could be summarized in a simple motto, *Ora et labora* ("prayer and work"), a reminder that the two activities together are complementary dimensions of a whole and holy life. But Benedict did more than prescribe a balance between work and prayer. The aim of monastic life is a state in which there is no artificial division between the sacred domain of prayer and the "worldly" activity of labor. Prayer is itself a form of work—the *opus dei* ("work of God")—while manual labor ideally should become a form of prayer.

How is this possible? How can work become a form of prayer? The connection is unclear as long as we think of prayer as something we do on our knees, preferably with eyes closed and hands folded neatly before us. In its basic sense, however, prayer is a matter of being present to God. It follows that if work is to assume a prayerful quality, there must be a spirit of work, a spirit of doing all things that similarly engages our hearts and places us in the presence of God.

It may be easier to imagine accomplishing this while washing dishes or watering the garden, tasks that require little mental concentration, but how do we maintain a consciousness of the presence of God while typing at a computer or operating heavy machinery? According to the monastic perspective, each task has its own good. When we work with proper attention and respect for that good, our work assumes a prayerful quality, and we can say that God is present in it. In contrast, a task performed carelessly, without respect for the good of the work, lacks the quality of prayer.

This theme was elaborated in one of the classics of Christian spirituality, *The Practice of the Presence of God*, a book drawn from letters and conversations with a French Carmelite lay brother in the seventeenth century. This man, known as Brother Lawrence of the Resurrection, entered a monastery in Paris in midlife, after retiring from long service in the army. Because of his peasant background and lack of formal education, he was assigned to kitchen work. There he spent forty years among the pots and pans until he died at the age of eighty. In his life he accomplished no great deeds. With the posthumous publication of his writings, however, he was recognized as one of the great spiritual masters of his age.

The title of his book neatly summarizes the substance of Brother Lawrence's spirituality. His spiritual method was simply to cultivate at all times a consciousness of the presence of God. By such an awareness, he believed, all our activities would be hallowed; we might find ourselves in a state of continuous prayer or "conversation with God." This was essentially a matter of acknowledging that God is *here*, *now*, in the task at hand. "The time of business," he wrote, "does not with me differ from the time of prayer; and in the noise and clatter of my kitchen, while several persons are at the same time calling for different things, I possess God in as great tranquility as if I were upon my knees at the Blessed Sacrament."

According to Brother Lawrence, there is no special distinction between traditional spiritual disciplines—reciting the Divine Office or worshiping in church—and the daily tasks with which he, for example, was chiefly occupied: scrubbing pots and chopping vegetables. The holiness of work, in other words, does not depend on the nature of the work but on one's own interior disposition. "Our sanctification," he wrote, "does not depend upon *changing* our works, but in doing for God's sake that which we commonly do for our own." For God, as he liked to observe, "regards not the greatness of the work, but the love with which it is performed."

Brother Lawrence's teaching helps bridge the gap between our image of "holy work," as performed by monks and nuns, and the mundane work of people in "the world"—whether stocking shelves at Wal-Mart, filing correspondence in an office, or painting yellow lines on the highway. In fact the saints were no strangers to "ordinary" work. They were teachers, nurses, and pot scrubbers like Brother Lawrence. They plowed fields, repaired churches with their bare hands, and balanced their accounts. Among their number—even if we allow that most canonized saints were clergy or members of religious orders—virtually every type of work has been represented. As a popular hymn puts it, "One was a doctor and one was a queen, and one was a shepherdess on the green. . . ."

For that matter one was a lawyer (Thomas More), one was a hairdresser (Pierre Toussaint), one was a vagabond (Benedict Joseph Labre), and at least one (as we have seen) spent his life perched on a pillar in the desert. All this only supports the observation of Meister Eckhart: "The kind of work we do does not make us holy, but we may make it holy."

In the end there is no such thing as "holy work." But at the same time there is no work—as long as it is not harmful or dishonest—that cannot be "hallowed," that cannot serve as a path to God, a way to happiness. Indeed it is possible to approach any form of labor as an opportunity for service or charity, as a setting for prayer or the chance to produce something beautiful, life-giving, and true.

Often such work goes unnoticed and unremarked. But occasionally one encounters people—a receptionist, a tollbooth operator, a checkout clerk in a grocery store—who perform their duties with such grace and love as to imbue their workplaces with an atmosphere of sanctity. Of such everyday saints, the above-cited hymn charmingly (if quaintly) proclaims: "You can meet them in school or in lanes, or at sea / in church, or in trains or in shops, or at tea."

On the question of work and holiness, Gerard Manley Hopkins, the nineteenth-century Jesuit poet, wrote: "When a man is in God's grace and free from mortal sin, then everything that he does, so long as there is no sin in it, gives God glory. . . . It is not only prayer that gives God glory but work. Smiting on an anvil, sawing a beam, whitewashing a wall, driving horses, sweeping, scouring, everything gives God some glory if being in his grace you do it as your duty. . . . To lift up the hands in prayer gives God glory, but a man with a dung fork in his hand, a woman with a slop-pail, gives him glory too. He is so great that all things give him glory if you mean they should."

The Shakers, a mysterious American sect that flourished in the United States in the nineteenth century, brought a similar worshipful attitude to all their work. Their legacy is preserved in barns, boxes, and furniture of simple beauty. As Thomas Merton observed of these products, "The peculiar grace of a Shaker chair is due to the fact that it was made by someone capable of believing that an angel might come and sit on it."

It makes quite a difference how we make a chair or set a table or serve a cup of coffee if we suspect that we might be (in St. Paul's phrase) "entertaining angels unawares." But the same goes for any task. St. Christopher, by legend, was a large man who made his living ferrying travelers across a river on his back. One night he was carrying a child who became so heavy that he could barely continue. "No wonder!" said the child. "You have been carrying the whole world. I am Jesus Christ, the king you seek!" How differently we would approach our common tasks—boring and burdensome as they may seem—if we believed our work were in service of the king we seek.

To be sure, in their quest for holiness, many saints did indeed give up some form of work, because it was wrong (as in the case of St. Martin of Tours, serving in the Roman army) or morally compromised (as in the case of St. Thomas More, chancellor of England) or because like St. Peter, they were called to labor in a wider field ("Follow me and I will make you a fisher of men"). But the call to holiness, as the saints have demonstrated, is no more a call to any particular work than a call to desist from work in general. It is rather a call to discover how in our work, our condition of life, we may find a way to praise God and thus to realize our vocation, our true path to happiness.

A CALLING

The word "vocation" comes from a Latin word for a summons or call. In everyday language the word has been sufficiently secularized so that it is often simply another term for our jobs or what we "do." In religious parlance, on the other hand, it has traditionally been identified with a particular calling: to the priesthood or monastic life. In this context, to speak of having a vocation means that one has decided to become a priest, a monk, or a nun.

But the lives of the saints show that the meaning of

"vocation" is both wider and narrower than that. Wider, because our calling (according to St. Paul) is ultimately to holiness itself, a calling not satisfied simply by our taking formal religious vows. It is at the same time narrower, in the sense that a vocation is ultimately a personal matter, addressed to a particular individual. It is the manner in which each of us is called to share in God's life.

Gerard Manley Hopkins invented a word, "selving," to describe the process of realizing and manifesting our unique and particular vocation. In the words of his poem "As kingfishers catch fire":

> Each mortal thing does one thing and the same:
>   Deals out that being indoors each one dwells,
>   Selves—goes itself; *myself* it speaks and spells,
> Crying *What I do is me: for that I came.*

For a kingfisher or a tree, such selving is more or less instinctive. As Thomas Merton put it, "A tree gives glory to God by being a tree. For in being what God means it to be it is obeying Him. It 'consents,' so to speak, to His creative love. It is expressing an idea which is in God and which is not distinct from the essence of God, and therefore a tree imitates God by being a tree." But what about human beings? Merton continues: "For me to be a saint means to be myself. Therefore the problem of sanctity and salvation is in fact the problem of finding out who I am and of discovering my true self."

That is why it is impossible fully to identify "vocation" with any particular work or state of life, as if finding a calling were like being matched with a prefitted suit of clothes. The struggle for many saints was to invent a path to holiness beyond the options available in their time: for St. Anthony, in the desert; for St. Benedict, in a monastery; for St. Francis and St. Clare, in radical poverty. All of them cleared the way for others to follow. But their invention grew from a prior rejection of the available alternatives. Something compelled them to seek a different way.

Charles de Foucauld (1858–1916), who began his life as a decadent French cavalry officer, later found his own way living as a hermit in Algeria. He sought to imitate the "hidden life" of Jesus, that major portion of Christ's life when he lived quietly as a carpenter in his hometown of Nazareth. As Foucauld put it, "God calls all the souls he has created to love him with their whole being, here and thereafter, which means that he calls all of them to holiness, to perfection, to a close following of him and obedience to his will. But he does not ask all souls to show their love by the same works, to climb to heaven by the same ladder, to achieve goodness in the same way. What sort of work, then, must *I* do? Which is *my* road to heaven? In what kind of life am *I to sanctify myself*?"

Foucauld's question is crucial. In what type of work, or place in life, may I find my *true self*, the person I am meant to be? As Merton wrote, "If we find that place we will be happy. If we do not find it we can never be completely happy."

The biblical pattern of vocation is suggested by those significant encounters between God and such figures as Noah, Abraham, Jacob, or Samuel, heroes of faith who heard themselves called by name and who responded, simply, "Here I am." In the Bible that recurring response invariably heralds a critical moment, not just the equivalent of shouting *"Present!"* during roll call. It represents the encounter in which a person's whole identity and sense of purpose are fused in response to a transcendent challenge.

But how does that challenge come to us today? As it did for Moses, from the midst of a burning bush? As it did for St. Francis, in a voice that spoke to him from a crucifix in a ruined chapel, charging him to "Repair my church"? As it did for many other saints, in hearing some message in scripture that seemed to single them out and grab them by the shoulders?

The lives of the saints appear to hinge on these decisive moments. But what distinguished the saints is not that they received *a call* from God, issued as often as not through the needs of a stranger or the moral challenge of the present moment. What was distinctive about the saints is that they heard the call as coming *from God* and therefore as one requiring a total response.

Naturally, it is easier to recognize such a call—when the time comes—if it takes the form of an answer to a previous question.

BODY AND SOUL

For Dorothy Day the question took shape in her as a child. She was born in Brooklyn in 1897, a daughter of an itinerant sportswriter. Though in her home God's name was never mentioned, she was attracted from an early age to the lives of the saints. She recalled being stirred by the stories of their charity toward the sick, the maimed, the leper. "But there was another question in my mind," she wrote. "Why was so much done in remedying the evil instead of avoiding it in the first place? . . . Where were the saints to try to change the social order, not just to minister to the slaves, but to do away with slavery?" Over time such questions caused her to shun religion and to place her hopes instead in the progressive politics of the day. Her friends were the Communists, Socialists, and anarchists with whom she worked on a variety of left-wing periodicals and in organizations like the Anti-Imperialist League.

Despite the excitement of such engagement with "history," Day's early life was also marked by loneliness and a kind of moral and spiritual confusion. By her own account, there was always a yearning for transcendence that distinguished her from her companions. One of them later remarked that she was "too religious" to make a good Communist. As she herself later reflected, borrowing words from a character in Dostoevsky, "All my life I have been haunted by God."

This yearning for the transcendent ultimately brought her to the Catholic church. Despite her experience of sorrow and disappointment, her conversion in the end was not prompted by sadness but by an experience of "natural happiness," the experience of pregnancy and giving birth to a daughter. She felt such joy and an impulse of gratitude so large, as she recalled it, that it could be directed only to God. Yet her conversion was an enormous leap, beyond the comprehension of her friends or the tolerance of her common-law husband (as she called him). An agnostic and anarchist, he disdained Catholicism and warned that her embrace of religion would put an end to their relationship. "It got to the point," she wrote, "where it was the simple question of whether I chose God or man."

Compounding this anguish, her decision to become a Catholic also seemed to involve a betrayal of the working class. On the one hand, she believed the Catholic church was the church of the poor, the masses, the immigrant. As her father put it scornfully, it was the church of "Irish cops and washerwomen." But to her radical friends—and to her as well—it seemed more often like a friend of the rich, a defender of the status quo.

She was at a loss about how to reconcile her nascent faith and her commitment to social justice. Following her baptism in 1927, she spent five lonely years in a kind of wilderness, supporting herself and her daughter, Tamar, on her uncertain income as a freelance writer, all the while praying that she might find a way of life "reconciling body and soul, this world and the next."

The answer came not in a voice from heaven but in the form of an unkempt man with a thick French accent, his pockets bulging with pamphlets and essays, whom she met one day in 1932. It was the Depression, and she had just returned from covering a Communist-organized march of the unemployed in Washington. The trip had represented a crisis in her search. In her anguish she had made her way to the National Shrine of the Immaculate Conception and prayed "that some way would open up for me to use what talents I possessed for my fellow workers, for the poor."

Soon after her return to New York Peter Maurin arrived at her door. He was a Frenchman of peasant roots, fifty-five years old, who had spent the previous twenty years tramping around the country, supporting himself by manual labor, all the while devising a unique vision of the gospel in action. He had received her name from a mutual acquaintance and determined, even before their meeting, that Day would be the one to put his vision to work.

Hardly waiting for an introduction, he commenced at

once to preach the ideas he had stored up. Maurin envisioned a movement—beginning with Day and himself—to implement the radical social message of the gospel. They would not simply *denounce* injustice, he said, but *announce* a new social order, based on a "philosophy of work" and the recognition of Christ in the poor. They would not wait for the church or the state to enact such a program. They would begin to live today according to their vision of the future, thus working to create a society in which "it would be easier for people to be good."

It took a while, more than one meeting, before Dorothy Day began to comprehend that this strange character was the answer to her prayer. But from that encounter, and in the movement that resulted, she found the work that engaged her for the rest of her life, nearly fifty years. The *Catholic Worker* newspaper was first distributed in Union Square on May 1, 1933 (the feast of St. Joseph the Worker). It became the organ of a movement centered in "houses of hospitality" across the country. In these Catholic Worker communities the traditional "works of mercy" (feeding the hungry, clothing the naked, sheltering the homeless) were joined with work for peace and social justice.

So Day found an answer to her childhood question, Where were the saints to change the social order? It was a question to be answered with her own life. By serving Christ in the poor, while battling injustice, and trying through small means to create a peaceful alternative, she found the meaning of her vocation. By inventing a new model of holiness, she found her own way to happiness.

The signs of a vocation are generally hidden in plain sight: within our own gifts and talents, the inner yearnings of our heart, that sense of what makes us feel most fully alive. When Flannery O'Connor was asked why she wrote short stories, she regularly replied, "Because I'm good at it." But the discernment of a vocation is just the beginning. The challenge remains, over a lifetime, to go deeper, to adjust course where necessary for the sake of remaining faithful. Indeed many saints have discovered what Mother Teresa of Calcutta, the most çelebrated saint of our time, described as a "call within a call."

By the time of her death in 1997 Mother Teresa's care for the destitute and dying people of Calcutta had made this small nun in her Indian garb a living icon of love and compassion. The celebrity of her later years tended to overshadow the many years of her life, up to the age of thirty-six, that she spent as an obscure Sister of Loretto from Albania, teaching geography in her order's schools in India. Throughout those years, though she was a devoted nun, loved by her students, there was nothing to suggest that she would emerge eventually as one of the great Christian witnesses of her age.

The turning point came one day in 1946, as she traveled by train to Darjeeling, a hill station in the Himalayas. On that day she suddenly received the conviction that God wanted something more from her: "He wanted me to be poor with the poor and to love him in the distressing disguise of the poorest of the poor." So, with the permission of her congregation, she left her convent. In place of her traditional religious habit she donned a simple white sari and went out to "seek Jesus" in the desperate byways of Calcutta. With nothing but five rupees to start with, she opened a home for the dying poor whose families had abandoned them in the streets. Eventually she was joined by others, including many of her former students. They became an international order, the Missionaries of Charity. Mother Teresa became a household name.

There is another word—"conversion"—that describes this process of going deeper. Typically, we reserve the term for the turning from sin. But so often in the stories of the saints the conversion in question is really a matter of finding their true calling. When that happens, their conversion amounts to a turn from listless anomie to a sense of joyous resolution. Where before life was weighted by the burden of mediocrity, now it is illuminated by a burning fire. Though perhaps they were already consecrated by religious vows, suddenly, with the discovery of a particular calling, their lives and work assume a new shape, a vitality and energy that were previously absent. It is this sense of vocation, the discovery of "*my* road to heaven," that transforms a work that is otherwise dull, onerous, or even repulsive, into a way of happiness. A Western journalist, watching Mother Teresa care for one of her dying charges, couldn't help observing, "I wouldn't do that for a million dollars." Mother Teresa replied, "Neither would I."

THE SEARCH FOR MEANING

Victor Frankl, a Jewish psychiatrist and survivor of the Holocaust, wrote a penetrating study based on his experiences in a concentration camp. In *Man's Search for Meaning* he described the origins of an approach to therapy based on what he termed the need for meaning. Such meaning might be found in a task, a value, or a commitment, but without it the human spirit withers. Of those in the camps who were to survive, he wrote: "We needed to stop asking about the meaning of life, and instead to think of ourselves as those who were being questioned by life—daily and hourly. Our answer must consist, not in talk and meditation, but in right action and in right conduct. Life ultimately means taking the responsibility to find the right answer to its problems and to fulfill the tasks that it constantly sets for each individual."

The problem of meaning may assume special urgency in the extreme conditions of a concentration camp. Ultimately, however, the need to respond to life's tasks and challenges confronts us all. Those who remain disengaged from these tasks become, like the bored and unhappy dinner guests in Tolstoy's story, prisoners of their own talk. In contrast, those who rise to the challenge can discover a type of happiness that endures—even in the midst of horrendous circumstances.

On December 2, 1980, a young Maryknoll sister named Ita Ford and three other North American churchwomen were abducted and killed by security forces in El Salvador. For nine months Ford had been part of a team of missioners working among refugees caught in the wake of civil war and a government-sponsored reign of terror. In El Salvador those who sided with the poor could expect, as Archbishop Oscar Romero put it, to meet the same fate as the poor: "to disappear, to be tortured, to be captive, and to be found dead." Ita Ford and her colleagues knew this. But earlier that summer Ford took a moment to write to her niece, Jennifer, a high school student in Brooklyn, on the occasion of her sixteenth birthday:

> This is a terrible time in El Salvador for youth. A lot of idealism and commitment are getting snuffed out here now. The reasons why so many people are being killed are quite complicated, yet there are some clear, simple strands. One is that people have found a meaning to live, to sacrifice, struggle, and even die. And whether their life spans sixteen years, sixty or ninety, for them their life has had a purpose. In many ways, they are fortunate people.
>
> Brooklyn is not passing through the drama of El Salvador, but some things hold true wherever one is, and at whatever age. What I'm saying is that I hope you can come to find that which gives life a deep meaning for you, something that energizes you, enthuses you, enables you to keep moving ahead.

Who does not wish to find that which gives life meaning, which enthuses us and enables us to keep moving ahead? For Tolstoy and the idealistic youth in his story, the key to happiness is simple in theory yet elusive in practice. It is a matter of detachment, work, and solidarity, all undertaken in a spirit of love. It compares in simplicity with Meister Eckhart's prescription for holiness: "Doing the next thing you have to do, doing it with your whole heart, and finding delight in doing it."

What do the saints teach us about work? On the one hand, they advise us of the importance of finding the path in life that is our own. Whether it is eminent or obscure, what matters is that it be *our own* way. On the other hand, there is the humbler discipline of finding the holiness that lies hidden in each particular work or task we undertake. In the words of Teilhard de Chardin, the Jesuit priest, mystic, and scientist, "God, in all that is most living and incarnate in him, is not far away from us, altogether apart from the world we see, touch, hear, smell and taste about us. Rather he awaits us every instant in our action, in the work of the moment. There is a sense in which he is at the tip of my pen, my spade, my brush, my needle. By pressing the stroke, the line, or the stitch, on which I am engaged, to its ultimate natural finish, I shall lay hold of that last end toward which my innermost will tends."

Here is where work enters into the saints' guide to happiness. To live and work with such a spirit is to aspire to be, like Ita Ford, one of those fortunate people who found their path, who knew what to look for and so found the strength to answer when they were finally called by name, "Here I am."

Four

LEARNING TO SIT STILL

Be still and know that I am God.   —Psalm 46

We cannot find God in noise or agitation. Nature: trees, flowers, and grass grow in silence. The stars, the moon, and the sun move in silence.   —Mother Teresa of Calcutta

THE REMOTE KINGDOM of Bhutan sits quietly in the shadow of the Himalayas. Some years ago the king of Bhutan made a curious pronouncement that attracted a good deal of attention. He declared that the national policy of his small Buddhist country was aimed not at increasing the gross national product but at increasing what he called gross national happiness. Whatever meaning this held for his subjects, it had the effect of attracting a great stream of foreign tourists and broadcast journalists, all eager to discover for themselves the secrets of the happy kingdom.

Many of these visitors returned with reports of a people who, though materially poor, do indeed display an evident contentment with life. While the Bhutanese lack many of the "benefits" of modern technology, they are not impoverished. In fact by certain criteria they enjoy an enviable prosperity.

For one thing, they have time on their hands, a commodity seldom reckoned by economists but apparently an important factor in computing "GNH."

If these residents of Bhutan were magically transported to downtown Manhattan, it is hard to say what they would observe with greatest interest. There are no Starbucks, let alone skyscrapers, in Bhutan. But perhaps nothing so exemplifies the ethos of our culture as the sight of people walking purposefully down crowded streets while conversing on mobile phones.

On the one hand, this phenomenon serves the principle that "Time is money." Not a moment should go to "waste." All the better if we can do two or three things at once. We can talk on the phone while driving a car or riding on a train. Thanks to mobile phones, instant messaging services, beepers, and call waiting, we are constantly available for interruption, whether in the middle of another conversation, while listening to a concert, while sitting in church, or even as we sleep. The telephone companies exclaim that now "we are all connected."

On the other hand, all this "connection" reflects a terrible desire to be somewhere else, anyplace but in the present moment.

We lack time. Yet it frightens us. We complain about the hectic pressures of our busy schedules. Still, it often seems that what we really miss is the time to do even more things. The prospect of long stretches of uninterrupted time, solitude, or quiet can be dreadful. Cancel all appointments, clear our schedules, and what would we rather do? Turn on the television, reach for a newspaper, pick up the phone, or plan some excursion that will leave us more exhausted than we were before.

There is of course a true spirit of leisure, just as there is a true spirit of work. But something else is going on when what really drives us is the need to avoid sitting still. Many prescriptions for happiness do no more than feed the constant craving for diversion. Is such "happiness" any more than a mask to disguise our true condition?

The saints accomplished many great works, whether managing schools and hospitals, ruling kingdoms, or simply conquering their own passions. But their action drew on a quality of stillness. True, they spent much of their time in prayer and contemplation. But in that quiet and stillness they found a peace that informed all their other work and activities.

Quiet places are becoming ever more scarce. But it is not enough simply to escape the noise of the world. There is still the matter of our own inner noise. Even when it is quiet outdoors, we are filled with internal voices and alarms, reminding us of what needs to be done, what we have done poorly, what has been done to us in the past. These voices incessantly distract us from the time and place—here and now—where we actually exist. They convince us that we will be happy in the future if only we can meet the next deadline, earn the proper credential, land the perfect job, or settle old scores. Yet if we are constantly living in the past or preparing to live in the future, how can we be sure that we are ever truly alive?

DISTRACTIONS

Our world provides ample opportunities for distraction and entertainment. But the hunger for diversion is not a recent phenomenon. It was the subject of acute analysis by the French philosopher and scientist Blaise Pascal, who lived in Paris in the seventeenth century. According to Pascal, "Sometimes, when I set to thinking about the various activities of men, the dangers and troubles that they face at Court, or in war, giving rise to so many quarrels and passions . . . I have often said that the sole cause of man's unhappiness is that he does not know how to stay quietly in his room."

Pascal was intimately familiar with Parisian society and its favored diversions: fancy balls, the latest style, gambling, gossip, and the hunt. From personal experience he had learned the limits of these worldly pastimes. "It is not that they really bring happiness, nor that anyone imagines that true bliss comes from possessing the money to be won at gaming or the hare that is hunted: no one would take it as a gift. What people want is not the easy peaceful life that allows us to think of our unhappy condition, nor the dangers of war, nor the burdens of office, but the agitation that takes our mind off it and diverts us. That is why we prefer the hunt to the capture."

In other words, the appeal of these activities is not that they bring happiness but that they offer distraction from our unhappiness. And so we embrace the opportunity to "push a ball with a billiard cue" or watch a dog in pursuit of a boar. That is apparently what it takes to forestall unhappiness—at least momentarily. According to Pascal, access to diversion is the principal attraction of wealth and power. A king, after all, has a large retinue "whose only thought is to divert him and stop him thinking about himself." But "leave a king entirely alone, with nothing to satisfy his senses, no care to occupy his mind, with no one to keep him company and no diversion, with complete leisure to think about himself, and you will see that a king without diversion is a very wretched man." What applies to a king is true for the regular run of humanity. No wonder that Pascal should exclaim, "How hollow and foul is the heart of man!"

Yet he was anything but a sour misanthrope. He was a man of boundless curiosity about the nature of reality, particularly as disclosed by the principles of mathematics. As a child prodigy he published studies on geometry. Before turning twenty, he had invented the calculating machine. He went on to lay the foundation for calculus, to perform original research on cones, prove the existence of vacuums, determine the weight of air, and design the first public transportation system in Paris. For the last of these achievements, the city of Paris honors him today as patron of the Métro.

But at a certain point Pascal's apprehension of reality was dramatically enlarged. He marked precisely the date and time—November 23, 1654, "from about half past ten in the evening until half past midnight"—when he had a deep mystical encounter with "the God of Jesus Christ." He recorded his impressions on a sheet of parchment, which he sewed into the lining of his jacket and kept on his person until the day he died, eight years later, at the age of thirty-nine. Fragmentary, like the most eloquent of his writings, his testament included these words: "Certainty, certainty, heartfelt, joy, peace. God of Jesus Christ . . . Joy, joy, joy, tears of joy."

Pascal did not speak about this experience. But from that time on he applied the same brilliance he had focused on cones and calculus to the problem of faith. In particular, he set out to write an ambitious defense of Christianity, addressed to the cultured skeptics of his time. The work was never completed; the manuscript exists only in a sketchy state, on scraps of paper strung together by bits of string.

Yet ironically, it is for this work, the *Pensées*, published after his death in 1662, that Pascal is best remembered.

Rather than begin his defense of Christianity—in the manner of traditional "apologetics"—with the testimony of scripture, the authority of the church, or the clockwork efficiency of creation, Pascal's plan was to start with the testimony of personal experience and the mysteries of the human heart. His whole work is structured around the dialectic of "wretchedness" and "happiness." He outlined his plan: "First part: Wretchedness of man without God. Second part: Happiness of man with God."

Wretchedness of man without God? The polite agnostics among Pascal's intended audience—the kind of people who dabbled in science and the latest intellectual fashions, who kept up with books and diverted themselves with tennis and gambling, exercise, and hobbies—would not instinctively count themselves among the wretched of the earth. But this was the starting point for Pascal's argument. It could be summarized in this lapidary characterization of the human condition: "Boredom, inconstancy, anxiety." On this basis Pascal addressed the human craving for diversion:

> We never keep to the present. We recall the past; we anticipate the future as if we found it too slow in coming and were trying to hurry it up, or we recall the past as if to stay its too rapid flight. . . . The fact is that the present usually hurts. . . . Let each of us examine his thoughts; he will find them wholly concerned with the past or the future. We almost never think of the present, and if we do think of it, it is only to see what light it throws on our plans for the future. The present is never our end. The past and the present

are our means, the future alone our end. Thus we never actually live, but hope to live, and since we are always planning how to be happy, it is inevitable that we should never be so.

Like St. Augustine before him, Pascal saw human beings as torn between a desire for happiness and an innate confusion about where to find it. The chief symptom of our wretchedness is simply our inability to sit still, to exist in the present moment. Instead we are forever seeking distraction in one thing or another. "If man were happy," he wrote, "the less he were diverted the happier he would be, like the saints and God."

It is easy to identify with Pascal's lament. Today the means of diversion are not merely more numerous but more sophisticated than in seventeenth-century France. One need not be a king to command an infinite range of distractions, all available at the push of a button. Computers, the Internet, CDs, DVDs, home entertainment systems, palm-size PlayStations—they are ubiquitous, all offering an effective defense against the prospect of solitude and silence. But what is so frightening about silence? Why is it so difficult to sit quietly in our room?

Perhaps it is not silence that worries us so much as the prospect of our own company. The capacity to sit alone in one's room without going mad implies the cultivation of an inner life. This is surely not the same as an "intellectual life," a capacity for learned thoughts. It is more a matter of resting in the core of one's being, what the desert fathers called the heart, or the soul. In a busy commercial culture, in contrast, everything encourages us to shun the inner life, to live on the surface, to satisfy our anxious cravings through the quick fix of consumption, distraction, the latest tabloid sensation, or the next big thrill.

Hence *"Inconstancy, boredom, anxiety,"* according to Pascal. As long as these are the sum of human life, it is vain to talk of happiness. But wretchedness did not have the last word in Pascal's scheme. The misery of human beings, he said, is the unhappiness of a dispossessed lord, a person in exile, for whom the memory of true happiness lingers on like an empty print or trace. Echoing St. Augustine, he wrote, "God alone is man's true good, and since man abandoned him it is a strange fact that nothing in nature has been found to take his place: stars, sky, earth, elements, plants, cabbages, leeks . . . since losing his true good, man is capable of seeing it in anything, even in his own destruction."

But there is a way out. For Pascal the attraction of Christianity lay first of all in its power to explain the human dilemma (that combination of greatness and wretchedness implied in the Christian stories of the creation and the fall) and second in the credibility of its solution. He believed that in Christ, who reveals both the depth of our disorder and the depth of God's love, we can find the way back to our true nature, our true home. The universe is no longer a cold, indifferent room from which we desperately seek escape. Resting in this mystery, we can sit in our rooms without dread, knowing that we are never truly alone, knowing with the saints what it might feel like to be truly happy.

THE BETTER WAY TO BE ALONE

It is interesting to imagine what Pascal would have made of Buddhism, a religion that has made a science out of sitting still. In Pascal's time, it was axiomatic that the truth of one's own religion must imply the falseness of all others. But more recently many Christians have drawn insights from such Eastern religious practices as Zen Buddhism, finding therein no necessary contradiction of their own faith. The distinctive feature of Zen practice is to sit still—though it is a very disciplined sort of sitting. Zen practitioners, sitting in stillness, paying attention to their breathing, aim at a state of mindfulness, an awareness of what it means to be fully alive in the present moment.

An ancient Buddhist sutra, "On Knowing the Better Way to Be Alone," describes an encounter between Buddha and a monk named Thera, who liked to live alone. After hearing from Thera a description of his life, Lord Buddha instructed him on "the better way to be alone": "It is the way of deep observation to see that the past no longer exists and the future has not yet come, and to dwell at ease in the present moment, free from desire. When a person lives in this way, he has no hesitation in his heart. He gives up all anxieties and regrets, lets go of all binding desires, and cuts the fetters which prevent him from being free."

The implication of this sutra is that there is no particular merit or value in simply being apart from other people, especially if we remain tossed by conflicting thoughts and desires. If it is to bring us happiness, the physical act of sitting quietly must be joined by a corresponding internal stillness or quiet.

The early desert monks treated this same topic. There were those who fled to the desert in search of peace and quiet only to be affronted by an array of "demons"—all the anger, impatience, and envy that had accompanied them on their retreat from the world. Long before the recent encounters with Eastern religion these Christian spiritual seekers invented their own version of "the better way to be alone." The desert fathers developed a practice of mindful prayer centered on the repetition of a holy phrase or even the name of Jesus. This practice became the basis of what was known as hesychasm, from the Greek *hesychia*, the word for "stillness" or "rest." In this case "stillness" referred to a spiritual discipline of interior prayer and rest in God.

The hesychasts took to heart St. Paul's exhortation to "pray always"—words literally translated as "come to rest." By constantly repeating the name of Jesus or the Jesus Prayer ("Lord Jesus Christ, Son of the Living God, have mercy on me, a sinner"), sometimes in coordination with the rhythm of their breathing, the monks entered a state of extreme concentration on spiritual reality. In such a state they liked to say that the Holy Spirit was praying through them. According to St. Gregory Palamas (d. 1359), a Greek monk of Mount Athos and one of the most famous proponents of this method, the Christian might, through this prayer, latch on to the divine nature, much like a rope flung over a rock, and thus pull free of worldly attachments and draw nearer to God.

The central texts of hesychastic spirituality were collected over the centuries in a volume titled *The Philokalia* (from the Greek, "love of beauty"). According to its modern editors, the purpose of *The Philokalia* was "to show the way to awaken and develop attention and consciousness, to attain that state of watchfulness that is the hallmark of sanctity." It was first published in Greek in the 1700s. Early in the next century a Slavonic edition appeared in Moscow. It was this book that inspired one of the classics of modern Russian spirituality, *The Way of a Pilgrim*.

This latter book, first published in Moscow in 1884, recounts the experience of an anonymous pilgrim of peasant origins who undertook a fantastic journey in the mid-nineteenth century, traversing the whole of Russia and Siberia on foot. He was introduced to *The Philokalia* by a holy monk from whom he had sought an explanation of St. Paul's words about unceasing prayer. The monk instructed him to begin by repeating the Jesus Prayer three thousand times a day. At first this required considerable effort. But within weeks the pilgrim had increased the observance to six thousand and then twelve thousand times a day. Soon, he wrote, "[m]y whole desire was fixed upon one thing only—to say the Prayer of Jesus. As soon as I went on with it I was filled with joy and relief. It was as though my lips and my tongue pronounced the words entirely of themselves without any urging from me. I spent the whole day in a state of the greatest contentment. . . . I lived as though in another world."

The prayer became his constant companion as he performed his daily routines and continued on his solitary way. Eventually he had the impression that the prayer had passed from his lips to his heart. At this point he found that he had no further need to repeat the words; they now coincided with the rhythm of his own breathing and the beating of his heart.

Despite the poverty and hardships of his life, the pilgrim discovered that through his unceasing "prayer of the heart," he was enabled to see the world by the light of the transfiguration. Not only did he feel that he was the happiest person on earth, "but the whole outside world also seemed to me full of charm and delight. Everything drew me to love and thank God; people, trees, plants, animals. I saw them all as my kinsfolk, I found on all of them the magic of the Name of God."

The Byzantine hesychasts on Mount Athos were dismissed by their critics as "navel gazers." To judge from the outside, it is easy to see how a spiritual discipline focused on one's breathing and the beating of one's heart might resemble the purest form of self-obsession. This was apparently the case with Franny Glass, the precocious college student in J. D. Salinger's *Franny and Zooey.* After reading *The Way of the Pilgrim*, she finds refuge from the world and the confusion of her life by locking herself in the bathroom and repeating the Jesus Prayer. Her brother Zooey brings her to her senses, criticizing her for using such a spiritual practice as a way of escaping the business of living—particularly the obligation to see Jesus in other people (including the hypothetical "fat lady" listening to her radio).

In the pilgrim's case, however, the achievement of an interior stillness—through the repetition of the Jesus Prayer—did not entail withdrawal from the world and its activities. Instead the world seemed somehow transparent. Whatever befell him—whether good fortune or ill—spoke to him of God. Every face reflected back to him the face of Christ. The result was a great happiness, which he eagerly shared with each person he encountered.

THE PRESENT MOMENT

In his commentary on the sutra "On Knowing the Better Way to Be Alone," the Vietnamese Zen master Thich Nhat Hanh notes the relation between happiness and being fully alive in the present moment. "To return to the present is to be in contact with life. Life can be found only in the present moment, because 'the past no longer is' and 'the future has not yet come.' Buddhahood, liberation, awakening, peace, joy, and happiness can only be found in the present moment. Our appointment with life is in the present moment. The place of our appointment is right here, in this very place."

Many people suppose that this Buddhist emphasis on the present moment contrasts with the Christian hope for eternal life. Some, like the French existentialist Albert Camus, have even criticized Christianity on this basis, charging that a preoccupation with the "afterlife" undermines our capacity for ethical engagement in the present. Doubtless, in their pursuit of holiness, many Christians have merited this criticism. But not all. Among the great saints and spiritual masters there are those who took a different approach. They believed that a hope in eternal life, far from rendering the present irrelevant, instead invests each moment with decisive significance.

Among their number was an eighteenth-century French Jesuit, Jean-Pierre de Caussade. His reputation rests entirely on a book published a full century after his death in 1751, *Abandonment to Divine Providence*. In reflections reminiscent of Brother Lawrence's *Practice of the Presence of God*, Caussade outlined the path to holiness that lies in the performance of our everyday tasks and duties. Every moment, according to Caussade, is given to us from God and so bears God's will for us. Thus, when we "accept what we cannot avoid, and endure with love and resignation things which cause us weariness and disgust," we are following the path to sanctification.

The words "the present moment" are central in Caussade's work. It is even legitimate, he claimed, to speak of the "sacrament of the present moment." Just as Christ, in the Eucharist, is visible to the eyes of faith under the appearance of bread, so to the faithful Christian it should be evident that God's will is truly present, though disguised, in what might otherwise be dismissed as ordinary and commonplace.

On one level Caussade's spirituality pertains to work and other activity. But on another it calls us to stillness and awareness. Caussade urged that we imagine each moment of our lives as a veil or shadow behind which the will of God awaits our discernment. To live in this consciousness is to awaken to the sacred depths of our existence. Acceptance of what God sends us in the present moment—this is the "mustard seed which is almost too small to be recognized or harvested, the treasure that no one finds, as it is thought to be too well hidden to be looked for. But what is the secret of finding this treasure? There isn't one. This treasure is everywhere. It is offered to us all the time and wherever we are."

Life inevitably supplies us with tedious situations: sitting in traffic, standing in line at the Department of Motor Vehicles, returning books to the library. But we needn't feel that these are interruptions or distractions from our spiritual practice. God's will is present in these moments, no less than in occasions of comfort and joy, perhaps calling us to greater patience, humility, and compassion.

Whatever the situation or the appropriate response, for Caussade the way of holiness lies in attention and obedience to God's will. But this is also, according to Caussade, the way to happiness. For by striving to live in such a spirit, despite all the apparent confusion and disorder of our lives, "we shall see all the loveliness and perfection of divine wisdom. Faith transforms the earth into paradise. By it our hearts are raised with the joy of our nearness to heaven.

Every moment reveals God to us." To live in such a way, for Caussade, is precisely the meaning of faith. Faith "tears aside the veil so that we can see the everlasting truth." If we do not live by such light, "we shall find neither happiness nor holiness, no matter what pious practices we adopt. . . ."

STABILITY

The Western monastic tradition has its own approach to sitting still—not so much in the literal sense of immobility as in the more figurative sense of being rooted. To the monastic vows of poverty, chastity, and obedience, St. Benedict introduced the vow of stability, the commitment, in principle, to remain in one's original monastery. Benedict scorned what he called "gyratory monks" who wandered restlessly from monastery to monastery, never making a commitment, "servants to the seduction of their own will and appetites." Absent such a commitment, according to this view, one is always tempted, when things become hard or boring, to seek out more congenial pastures.

Of course an aversion to commitment is not the sole property of gyratory monks; there are some people, for example, who indefinitely postpone making a commitment to others in marriage. They suffer from the apprehension that such a step will foreclose other options: What if I marry someone today only to find, tomorrow or the next year, someone else who suits me "better"? Meanwhile there are those who enter such relationships while mentally "keeping their options open." With this attitude it becomes easier, when times are difficult, to exercise the escape clause. After all, we have simply married "the wrong person." Similarly, absent the vow of stability, we might easily blame the inevitable difficulties of monastic life on the shortcomings of our abbot or the stupidity of our fellow monks and so imagine taking off after some place more sympathetic and better suited to our "needs."

The imperfection of human nature means that in reality there is no "perfect partner" or "perfect community." To be sure, there is such a thing as the wrong situation, just as there are unhealthy and destructive relationships. But if we are beset by the anxiety that somewhere, out there, better options await us, we shall not be really happy. Nor shall we attain our full measure as human beings as long as we glide over life, never touching the ground or planting roots. As long as we are constantly attuned to the happiness that awaits us over the rainbow we shall be oblivious of the happiness at hand. And as Pascal noted, since we are always dreaming of happiness in the future, it follows that we shall never be happy in the present, the moment in which we actually live.

The desert monastics had a name for this kind of restless depression. They called it acedia. We might call it the inability to sit still. In a classic description of this condition, the monk Evagrius Ponticus wrote:

> The demon of *acedia*—also called the noonday demon—is the one that causes the most serious trouble of all. . . . First of all he makes it seem that the sun barely moves, if at all, and that the day is fifty hours long. Then he constrains the monk to look constantly out the windows, to walk outside the cell, to gaze carefully at the sun to determine how far it stands from the ninth hour, to look now this way and now

that to see if perhaps one of the brethren appears from his cell. Then too he instills in the heart of the monk a hatred for the place, a hatred for his very life itself, a hatred for manual labor. . . . He depicts life stretching out for a long period of time, and brings before the mind's eye the toil of the ascetic struggle and, as the saying has it, leaves no leaf unturned to induce the monk to forsake his cell and drop out of the fight.

As another desert father observed, "When [acedia] besieges the unhappy mind, it begets aversion from the place, boredom with one's cell, and scorn and contempt for one's brethren. . . . We praise other and far distant monasteries, describing them as more helpful to one's progress, more congenial to one's soul's health."

Thomas Merton's journals make it clear that this "noonday demon" haunted even the best-known monk of the twentieth century. Merton's autobiography, *The Seven Storey Mountain*, and his early monastic writings described a feeling of giddy homecoming. In the Trappist monastery of Gethsemani he had found what he called the "center of America," his own road to happiness. But his later journals told a different story: irritation with the banal business operations of the monastery; conflicts with the abbot; frustration with a religious system that seemed determined to stifle his yearnings for a life of solitary prayer.

With growing intensity he was beset by the notion of joining a "purer" order, the Carthusians or the Camaldolese. This gave way to fantasies of fleeing to a hermitage or a community in Mexico, Nicaragua, Chile, New Mexico, or Alaska. Letters were written to Rome. Airline schedules were consulted. Plans for new foundations, as to diet, schedule of prayer, manner of work, etc., were spelled out. Inevitably these plans were quashed by his superiors, if they had not already been replaced by newer schemes.

Eventually Merton was given permission to live in a simple hermitage on the monastery grounds, a situation that proved conducive to both prayer and creative work. And though a more permissive abbot did finally allow him to travel outside the monastery—ultimately in 1968 to the conference in Bangkok where he died in an electrical accident—he had by then found peace with his vocation and his vow of stability. Gethsemani was, after all, his home, his arena for sanctity, the place, he was convinced, where he had been called to work out his salvation.

Of course the vow of stability makes sense only in the context of what Benedict called *conversatio morum*—roughly, the "conversion of manners"—an ongoing process of growth and spiritual maturity. There is no particular virtue in simply staying put for a lifetime in a job or a relationship in which we make ourselves and everyone around us miserable. Monastic stability is related to the monks' shared accountability to one another and to God. It makes sense and finds its spiritual value when it joins a commitment to seek out the depths—to strive for the hidden heart or soul of one's vocation and situation in life.

The desert fathers were experts in the rhythms and seasons of monastic life; they knew that the experience of consolation is as variable as the moon. As a result, they were compassionate about what they termed the perturbations of the heart. Their prescribed remedies might take the form of work, perseverance in prayer, or renewed discipline. The counsel of Evagrius, however, is particularly poignant: "When we meet with the demon of *acedia*, then is the time with tears to divide our soul in two. One part is to encourage; the other is to be encouraged."

A STILL VOICE

A saint is someone who has acquired a taste for the holiness of God, a person whose heart has become attuned to the rhythm of love. It is difficult to hear that rhythm amid the noise and commotion of daily life. It requires a certain space and silence and time devoted to listening.

Many saints, burdened like the rest of us by deadlines and responsibilities, found it difficult to find that external space. And so they fashioned their own "interior castle." This is what St. Catherine of Siena, a medieval Italian mystic and prophet, did when her family resisted her desire to enter a convent. After her father locked her up in their house and forced her to assume the duties of a servant, Catherine responded by constructing "an oratory in her heart"—a place of silent prayer—to which she could retreat in the midst of her daily chores. Outwardly she was immersed in the bustle and commotion of a busy household. But all the while her true life found shelter in her own secret chamber. In this way, as she later reflected, she transformed her daily tasks and duties into a ladder to heaven.

In one of the most mysterious stories in the Bible (1 Kings 19:11–12) the prophet Elijah, hiding from those who would take his life, found refuge in a cave where he awaited some word from the Lord. "And behold, the Lord passed by, and a great and strong wind rent the mountains, and broke in pieces the rocks before the Lord, but the Lord was not in the wind." Nor it turns out, was the Lord in a subsequent earthquake or in the great fire that followed. But after the fire Elijah heard "a still small voice."

It takes discernment to know that God's voice is not in an earthquake or in a mighty fire or a ferocious wind. But to hear the word of God in a still small voice requires more than just discernment. It also requires a modicum of silence.

Typically, we rely on the world to protect us from this silence. Above all, the noise of the world and its many opportunities for distraction help us avoid the terrifying silence of our own inner spaces. But we pay a price: inconstancy, boredom, anxiety. In contrast, the happiness of the saints presupposes a degree of inwardness—simply, the capacity for an interior life. How do we develop interior lives if we live entirely on the surface?

The great masters of prayer have compared the spiritual life to an ocean. On the surface life may be roiled by wind and tides. Yet beneath the surface, even amid a stormy sea, the water is calm. The pursuit of happiness is anchored in those depths.

Five

LEARNING TO LOVE

Beloved, let us love one another, for love is of God, and he who loves is born of God and knows God. He who does not love does not know God; for God is love. —1 John 4:7–8

Love is patient and kind; love is not jealous or boastful; it is not arrogant or rude. Love does not insist on its own way; it is not irritable or resentful; it does not rejoice at wrong but rejoices in the right. Love bears all things, believes all things, hopes all things, endures all things. —1 Cor. 3:4–7

WILLIAM BLAKE, the English poet and visionary artist, left a concise definition of the path to holiness. He wrote, "We are put on earth for a little space, that we may learn to bear the beams of love." Blake, who regularly conversed with angels in his garden, was equally eccentric in matters spiritual and artistic. Yet his statement accords with the wisdom of the saints. They all have agreed that sanctification is a matter of being conformed to God—of steadily "putting off the old person and putting on Christ," whose nature is simply love itself.

Scripture teaches that human beings are created in the image of God. This is another way of saying that we are created in the image of love, so that we are never so truly ourselves as when we reflect that image. But what do we really know about love? Most of us consider ourselves fortunate to have loved a few people deeply in our lives, whether parents, partners, children, or friends. We are expected, by popular culture, to measure those loves against the search for that one person, somewhere, destined to be "the love of our life." But according to the saints, there is a greater measure.

Nothing is so deeply fixed in our hearts as the longing to love and to be loved. Songs and poems and greeting cards tell us the same, that "love is all you need." Does that mean that on this point, at least, the saints have agreed with the Beatles? Perhaps so. But Blake's words point to something more than simply the gratification of our "heart's desire." They direct us to a steady process of growth and conversion. What is at stake is not simply the fulfillment of our longing but the need to enlarge, by degrees, our very capacity to love; to be conformed to the love, as Dante put it, that "moves the Sun and the other stars."

Our task on earth is to learn to bear the beams of love. If we accomplish this, whether our lives are long or short, we shall have realized the purpose of our existence; we shall have achieved the happiness of the saints. We shall have known that "mirth in the love of God" that Richard Rolle, an English mystic of the fourteenth century, attributed to holy people. "If our love be pure and perfect," he said, "whatever our hearts love, it is God."

IN LOVE

What do we know about love? Poets have always sung its praises, describing its power to make us feel more alive, to become so absorbed in the good of another as to lose all sense of a separate identity, to be willing "to bear all things, hope all things, endure all things" for the sake of our beloved. To one who is "in love" the world looks different. What seemed dull and gray takes on color. Life has a purpose and promise. What appeared closed is suddenly open. We are no longer alone, for there is someone who shares our joys and sorrows, someone who knows the secrets of our hearts. And we wish to be worthy of this gift. As Jack Nicholson, in the role of a supremely neurotic character in *As Good As It Gets*, remarks to the character played by Helen Hunt, "You make me want to be a better man."

With so many films and sonnets and songs to draw on, what more can we possibly learn from the saints? Not much, we might suppose, if we share the assumption that holy people occupy some spiritual zone beyond the reach of ordinary human feelings. St. Thérèse of Lisieux said that the mission of her short life was simply to "make Love loved," which sounds ambitious—yet abstract. Forced to choose between a love for "Love" itself and the love of a dog, a cat, or any sympathetic companion, many people might settle for what they can actually touch. Is the saint's version of love, in that case, merely an ethereal, bloodless shadow of the "real thing"?

This question only shows how much there is to learn about reality itself. For the sake of loving God, the saints did not forswear the love of other people, places, or things that made them happy. Quite the contrary. They believed that love is a key. But behind each door it opens there is another that leads to something wider.

The saints were the last ones to settle for a world of shadows and evasion. It is they who pursued the trail of our humanity to its source in a reality that is progressively larger and deeper. They believed that all love, all beauty, all happiness in this life are a sample and foretaste of the "real thing." In this light, St. Augustine wrote:

> What do I love when I love my God? Not material beauty or beauty of a temporal order; not the brilliance of earthly light, so welcome to our eyes. . . . And yet, when I love him, it is true that I love a light of a certain kind, a voice, a perfume, a food, an embrace; but they are of the kind that I love in my inner self, when my soul is bathed in light that is not bound by space; when it listens to sound that never dies away; when it breathes fragrance that is not borne away on the wind; when it tastes food that is never consumed by the eating; when it clings to an embrace from which it is not severed by fulfillment of desire. This is what I love when I love my God.

One need not be a saint in order to love. But it would appear that only someone who has loved can be a saint.

NATURAL HAPPINESS

Maybe St. Augustine is not the most helpful example. In the early chapters of his *Confessions* he refers frequently to his desperate search for "some object for my love." In different forms and persons, including his mistress of many years, he evidently found it. But in every case Augustine wants to show how the "clear waters" of love were invariably spoiled by the "black river of lust." He describes his relationship with his unnamed mistress, the mother of his son, in these unflattering terms: "In those days I lived with a woman, not my lawful wedded wife, but a mistress whom I had chosen for no special reason but that my restless passions had alighted on her."

Augustine's treatment stands in marked contrast with a similar passage in Dorothy Day's memoir, *The Long Loneliness*, in which she introduces the story of her love for a man named Forster and the role he played in hastening her spiritual journey: "The man I loved, with whom I entered into a common-law marriage, was an anarchist, an Englishman by descent, and a biologist." She met him at a party in Greenwich Village in the early 1920s. Soon afterward they began to live together—as Day put it, "in the fullest sense of the phrase"—in a house on Staten Island, paid for by her sale of movie rights to an autobiographical novel.

Among their bohemian set there was nothing scandalous about such a relationship. It was evidently Day who liked to think of it as a "common-law marriage." For Forster, who never masked his scorn for the "institution of the family," their relationship was simply a "comradeship." Nevertheless, she loved him "in every way." She wrote: "I loved him for all he knew and pitied him for all he didn't know. I loved him for the odds and ends I had to fish out of his sweater pockets and for the sand and shells he brought in with his fishing. I loved his lean cold body as he got into bed smelling of the sea and I loved his integrity and stubborn pride." As for Forster's feelings, "He loved nature with a sensuous passion and he loved birds and beasts and children because they were not men."

It was during this time of "natural happiness," as she called it, that she found herself imagining an even greater happiness. Forster's ardent love of creation made him disdainful of religion, but for her it had the opposite effect, bringing her instead "to the Creator of all things." She began praying during her walks and even attending mass. "How can there be no God, when there are all these beautiful things?" she challenged Forster. But there was a widening gulf between them.

All this occurred even before her pregnancy and the birth of her daughter, an event that crystallized her religious yearnings. She determined that she would have her child baptized, "cost what it may." The cost was high. She could not become a Catholic while maintaining this "common-law marriage." Forster, for his part, would have nothing to do with a wedding, either civil or religious. With great pain, they parted ways.

Maybe Dorothy Day is not a good example either. Her story, like Augustine's, might appear to demonstrate the conflict between "merely" human love and "higher" religious aspirations. But that is not how Day saw it. "I could not see that love between man and woman was incompatible with love of God," she wrote. "God is the Creator, and the very fact that we were begetting a child made me have a sense that we were made in the image and likeness of God, co-creators with him." Her account of this story has none of Augustine's obligatory expressions of shame and regret. It is a story of how, "through a whole love, both physical and spiritual," she came to know God.

But this was not the end of her story. Her experience of "natural happiness" had stimulated her thirst for a greater happiness. Her love for Forster, for her daughter, for the beauty of the earth, and her love too for the poor and downtrodden had brought her to believe in an even greater love. All this, after her meeting some years later with Peter Maurin, she would carry with her into the Catholic Worker.

St. Augustine called life a "road of the affections," a process of learning what is worthy of our love and how to love appropriately. Many people live enclosed in their own self-love, a prison defined by the limits of their comfort, possessions, or reputation. Others extend the walls somewhat farther to include one other person or a chosen few. Some draw the boundary around their family, their country, or their church. All these have their value. The question is whether we are open to the voice that calls us deeper. When love is the horizon and not the boundary of our existence, then all things reveal their hidden depth and draw us onward. Not simply all that is beautiful but even the commonplace and routine, things accounted as poor and worthless, can serve as windows on the infinite.

GOD AND OUR NEIGHBOR

Asked to name the greatest of the commandments, Jesus provided an answer in two parts. On the one hand, he said, we must love God with our "whole heart, and whole mind, and strength and soul." But immediately this was linked to a second commandment, "like unto the first," that we should love our neighbor as ourselves. As an example of what this meant in practice Jesus offered the story of a Samaritan, an adherent of a sect despised by orthodox Jews, who interrupted his journey to care for a stranger he found lying naked and injured at the side of the road.

On this subject, Sigmund Freud observed that the commandment to "love one's neighbor as oneself" is a vain and nonsensical statement that simply functions, in its impossibility, as an inducement to guilt. Yet what was folly to Freud is comprehensible enough to most parents. To have a child is to recognize just how possible it is to love another person "as oneself." Evolutionary psychology may go some way toward explaining these feelings. But not all the way. There are many other examples of people who have responded to the needs of others with just such a fierce, protective love.

There is, for instance, St. Maximilian Kolbe, a Franciscan priest who volunteered in Auschwitz to take the place of another prisoner condemned to death. (The man he saved was alive forty-one years later to attend his canonization.) Or Damien of Molokai, the Belgian priest who lived among the lepers in an isolated colony in Hawaii until he succumbed to their disease. Or for that matter, Oskar Schindler, the German industrialist in Poland who faced great peril to rescue his Jewish factory workers from the Holocaust. Schindler's example is striking precisely because he was apparently not, at least by conventional standards, a "good man," much less a candidate for canonization.

Such examples may represent the far end of the moral spectrum. Perhaps Christ's standard for loving God and our neighbors is simply a horizon toward which we strive, usually falling short. But if "our whole heart, our whole mind, and strength and soul" sets the bar too high, the fact remains that Jesus provided a simpler test. In the Gospel of Matthew he described how the day of judgment will hang on these words: "I was hungry and you gave me food . . . I was a stranger and you welcomed me, I was sick and you visited me." We ask: When did we do these things? And here Jesus discloses the secret meaning of the parable of the Good Samaritan: "Insofar as you did these things to the least of these, you did them to me" (Matt. 25:31–46).

The saints have lived by the implications of this mystical symmetry. They believed that Jesus appears to us in a neighbor: the stranger, forever naked and bleeding on the side of the road; the sick person who needs our care; the hungry person with whom we share our bread; the lonely one whose burden we ease. Yet from without, the equation does indeed appear vain and nonsensical: on the one hand, a ragged beggar; on the other, the Son of God. It is love that balances the scale. For want of that love, we all are ragged beggars. As Mother Teresa wrote, "God has identified himself with the hungry, the sick, the naked, the homeless; hunger, not only for bread, but for love, for care, to be somebody to someone; nakedness, not of clothing only, but nakedness of that compassion that very few people give to the unknown; homelessness, not only just for a shelter made of stone, but that homelessness that comes from having no one to call your own."

And so, in an absolute sense, whether we travel by loving God or loving our neighbors, ultimately we come to the same end. Whenever we give without counting the cost or calculating the return, we are learning to bear the beams of love.

LOVE AND HAPPINESS

But does love make us happy?

The answer depends in part on what we mean by love

and what we mean by happiness. Again, for Freud, it is an illusion to think they are connected. "We are never so defenseless against suffering as when we love," he wrote, "never so helplessly unhappy as when we have lost our loved object or its love." According to this view, love is an acquisitive instinct that seeks an object to grasp and keep. Any happiness based on love is necessarily fragile since we cannot truly possess the heart of another.

That undoubtedly describes a certain kind of love. But the saints had something else in mind. One of the paradoxes of the gospel is the teaching that we truly possess only what we give away. Love that hinges on the expectation of return is simply the law of the marketplace or what Simone Weil liked to call gravity. True love defies the laws of gravity; it does not express itself through grasping, but through freely giving.

The same is true of happiness. As Thomas Merton wrote, "A happiness that is sought for ourselves alone can never be found: for a happiness that is diminished by being shared is not big enough to make us happy. There is a false and momentary happiness in self-satisfaction, but it always leads to sorrow because it narrows and deadens our spirit. True happiness is found in unselfish love, a love that increases in proportion as it is shared."

Charles Dickens's "A Christmas Carol" offers a familiar treatment of this theme. Ebenezer Scrooge, a wealthy miser, is hardly aware of his own unhappiness until a series of apparitions helps him review the desert of his life. In observing a sequence of tableaux drawn from Christmases past, present, and future, he confronts the barrenness of his own life and recognizes the wider web of human relations in which each person is embedded. He sees the effects of his actions and attitudes on the happiness of others. He sees how his own rejection of love in the past has frozen his own capacity for life. He notices, as if for the first time, the reality of the lives around him, the suffering that he has failed to avert, the opportunities for love that he has squandered. Finally he glimpses the fate that awaits him, to die alone with his wealth, unloved and unmourned. Convicted by this vision, Scrooge embraces the opportunity to change his life. Now, living in the true spirit of Christmas, he realizes what it means to love. This, in turn, transforms the appearance of the world around him. "He went to church, and walked about the streets, and watched the people hurrying to and fro, and patted children on the head, and questioned beggars, and looked down into the kitchens of houses, and up to the windows, and found that everything could yield him pleasure. He had never dreamed that any walk—that anything—could give him so much happiness."

A life in which there is no breath of love is a miserable existence. Like a plant without sufficient water, it may exist in some desiccated state, but it cannot flourish. At the same time, there is at the center of each of us a secret identity, unknown even to ourselves, that lies sleeping, awaiting the kiss of the beloved to awaken at last. That kiss may take many forms. Sometimes it is the love of another person whose existence invites us into a world that is suddenly noble and beautiful. For St. Francis of Assisi it was the kiss of a leper. For St. Antony it was a reading from scripture that stirred him as never before. For St. Catherine of Genoa it was the sense of being truly forgiven. However love enters our lives, it calls us to our better selves, makes us braver, kinder, more forgiving, more ashamed of our failures, more resolute in our efforts to improve.

In the Gospel of Luke, Jesus observes a man named Zacchaeus who has climbed a sycamore tree to get a better view
over the crowd. Zacchaeus is a short man, but he has another reason for observing from afar. He is a tax collector, a
man disdained by his neighbors as a social parasite. Nevertheless, from the midst of the crowd Jesus calls him down
from his sycamore tree, addressing him by name: "Zacchaeus, make haste and come down; for I must stay at your
house today." The crowd mumbles scornfully; Zacchaeus is
a sinner. But Zacchaeus is so moved by this personal attention that he responds with a bold public declaration: He will
change his life; he will give half his property to the poor;
he will restore the goods of anyone he has defrauded
(Luke 19:1–8).

Many of the saints could identify with that man in the
sycamore tree. Like Zacchaeus, they had the experience of
being known and loved by God. In this love they found the
courage to start anew, to do impossible things, to become
different people. As St. John the Evangelist wrote, "We love,
because he first loved us" (1 John 4:19).

Even in its familiar everyday forms, love bears the power
to transform and redeem. Dostoevsky depicts this power in
Crime and Punishment. At the end of his novel the mur-
derer Raskolnikov has been sent to Siberia. A broken, disil-
lusioned man, his nihilistic creed has brought him to the
dead end of prison exile. But it is not a dead end, after all.
Sonia, a prostitute, has come to join him in voluntary exile.
It was she who had previously urged him to confess his
crime and cleanse his soul. Doubtless, she sees in him now
the possibility of her own new start. Meanwhile her patient
love seeks out the spark of his soul and fans it to life. Earlier
in the novel, in a particularly moving scene, Sonia had read

to Raskolnikov the gospel story of the raising of Lazarus. Now, under the influence of her love, another resurrection occurs: "They wanted to say something, but could not. Tears came. They were both pale and thin; yet in those pale, sickly faces there already glowed the light of the renewed future, resurrection to a new life. Love resurrected them; the heart of one contained infinite sources of life for the heart of the other. They resolved to wait and be patient. There were seven years to go; and until then how much unbearable pain, what infinite happiness!"

"Hell is not to love anymore," says the hero of Georges Bernanos's *Diary of a Country Priest*. Yet the "lowest of human beings, even though he no longer thinks he can love, still has in him the power of loving." It is this power of loving, lost and forgotten though it may be, that forms the precious core, the soul, of every person. Whatever is implied by the word "salvation," it always involves the rediscovery and cultivation of that latent power. Something precious was lost and now it is found. When this occurs, another Lazarus rises again.

LOVE IN ACTION

The songs on the radio eloquently describe the *feelings* of love—the yearning, the burning desire. Christian mystics have adopted this very language to describe the relationship between God and the soul. As St. Teresa of Ávila described it, that relationship "is like the experience of two persons here on earth who love each other deeply and understand each other well; even without signs, just by a glance, it seems, they understand each other. These two lovers gaze directly at each other." Drawing on the imagery of the biblical Song of Songs, she wrote, "My Lord, I do not ask you for anything else in life but that *You kiss me with the kiss of your mouth,* and that you do so in such a way that although I may want to withdraw from this friendship and union, my will may always, Lord of my life, be subject to Your will and not depart from it; that there will be nothing to impede me from being able to say: 'My God and my Glory, indeed *Your breasts are better and more delightful than wine.*' "

The saints, it appears, were not insensible to feelings. But they also knew that love is about more than words and feelings. Whether it is in loving one's spouse, "neighbor," or even one's enemy, love reveals itself in action.

In *The Brothers Karamazov,* Dostoevsky offered a telling reflection on this point through the character of Father Zossima, a holy abbot, whose teachings provide the spiritual center for the novel. In one memorable scene, Zossima attempts to counsel a proud and wealthy woman who has sought his advice. She tells him that she suffers from a lack of faith: What if there is no eternal life?

No one can prove the existence of the hereafter, he replies, but one *can* be convinced. How? "By the experience of *active love,*" he instructs her. "Strive to love your neighbors actively and indefatigably. And the nearer you come to achieving this love, the more convinced you will become of the existence of God and the immortality of your soul. If you reach the point of complete selflessness in your love of your neighbors, you will most certainly regain your faith and no doubt can possibly enter your soul."

Active love? This raises another difficulty for Zossima's visitor. "You see," she says, "I love humanity so much that—would you believe it? I sometimes dream of giving up all, all I have . . . and becoming a hospital nurse. I close my eyes, I think and dream and at those moments I feel full of indomitable strength." There is only one problem: What if the patients are not grateful? She feels she could stand anything but ingratitude.

To this Father Zossima offers the penetrating reply, "Love in action is a harsh and dreadful thing compared to love in dreams."

We do not learn to love by daydreaming. We learn to love by loving. In the words of Theophan the Recluse, one of the early desert fathers, "You say that you have no humility or love. So long as these are absent, everything spiritual is absent. . . . Humility is acquired by acts of humility, love by acts of love." Acts of love, repeated daily, establish the habit of love. What begins with a conscious effort may become, with practice, a certain attitude toward life. As our character is molded by charity, it forms our response to every situation and encounter.

And what if the people we love are not grateful? Then we may heed the advice of St. John of the Cross: "Where there is no love, put love, and you will draw love out."

THE ART OF LOVING

Still, it is difficult, indeed "unnatural," to love those who do not love us in return. It is easy here to speak of the role of grace. But grace is not the same as Cupid's arrow. Choice and discipline play their part. There is such a thing, as Erich Fromm put it, as "the art of loving."

St. Thérèse of Lisieux (1873–1897), who spent most of her short life in a Carmelite convent in Normandy, was an adept practitioner of this art. Early in life Thérèse determined that she would become a saint, and even as a child she had devised her method. She called it "the way of spiritual childhood" or "the Little Way." It was based on an attitude of total trust in God, an effort to respond with love to each chore, encounter, or petty insult that made up her daily life. She believed that by the practice of this discipline she could take the ordinary business of life and convert it into the fuel of love. Every situation might become an arena for holiness. And by the small, molecular influence of each action and intention, she might help transform the world.

Despite her sentimental language—she liked to call herself a "little flower" in God's garden and a "plaything to the Child Jesus"—Thérèse possessed an iron will, an absolute determination to achieve her goal. It was not a modest goal. In her autobiography, published after her death as *The Story of a Soul*, she confessed to feeling a call to every vocation, to be a warrior, a priest, a doctor of the church, and a martyr. But ultimately she believed that her vocation was nothing less than to "love itself," a virtue embracing every calling without exception. "My vocation is love!" she wrote. "In the heart of the Church, who is my Mother, *I will be love.*" This conviction brought her joy, though it came at a price. In Thérèse's case the "little way," her road to holiness, included all the daily pinpricks of community life: the sister with an annoying way of fidgeting with her rosary or the one who inadvertently splashed dirty water on her while doing the laundry. Each of these was an occasion to restrain the impulse to judgment and resentment, to enlarge her capacity for patience and forgiveness. Of course, as she observed, in a convent "one has no enemies, but one certainly has natural likes and dislikes. One feels attracted to a certain Sister and one would go out of one's way to dodge meeting another. Jesus tells me that it is this very Sister I must love, and I must pray for her even though her attitude makes me believe she has no love for me." Quoting scripture, she noted, "If you love them that love you, what thanks are to you? For sinners also love those that love them."

Ultimately Thérèse's sufferings amounted to considerably more than the "pinpricks" of community life. After contracting a virulent form of tuberculosis, she spent her final months in agony of body and spirit. Toward the end, she said, she faced every form of temptation, including the specter of despair. But she held fast to her method, convinced that in this faithfulness lay the arena for her witness and the guarantee of her eventual victory.

One day, as one of the sisters read to her about eternal happiness, she suddenly said: "It is not that which attracts me. It is love! To love and be loved!, and to return to earth to make Love to be loved!" In her final weeks she returned to this theme again. "I feel that my mission is about to begin," she said, "my mission of making souls love the good God as I love Him, to teach my little way to souls. If my desires receive fulfillment, I shall spend my heaven on earth even until the end of time. Yes, I will spend my heaven doing good upon earth."

Thérèse was only twenty-four when she died. Nevertheless, her message soon found an enormous audience around the world. Indeed, following her canonization, she became one of the most popular saints of modern times. In part, this reflected the universality of her "Little Way." There may be few who are called to do great things, to witness before princes, or to shoulder the cross of martyrdom. Yet as Thérèse demonstrated, there is a principle of continuity between our response to the everyday situations in which we find ourselves and the "great" arenas in which the saints and martyrs offered their witness. According to Thérèse, each moment, accepted and lived in a spirit of love, is an occasion for heroism and a step along the path to happiness and holiness.

CHOOSING TO LOVE

Though she was, by coincidence, born in the year of Thérèse's death, 1897, Dorothy Day would otherwise appear to have little in common with "the Little Flower." In fact her own first impression of the saint was unfavorable. She received a copy of Thérèse's autobiography from her confessor in 1928, soon after her conversion, and found it "colorless, monotonous, too small in fact for my notice." As she later wrote, "What kind of saint was this who felt that she had to practice heroic charity in eating what was put in front of her, in taking medicine, enduring cold and heat, restraint in enduring the society of mediocre souls, in following the strict regime of the Carmelite nuns which she had joined at the age of fifteen?" A reformer like Teresa of Ávila or a champion of justice like Joan of Arc—these were the kinds of saints who appealed to her. The story of Thérèse, in contrast, struck her as "pious pap." Yet over time Day was to embrace Thérèse as her favorite saint, going so far as to write a book about her life and the spirituality of the "Little Way." Day was among the few to recognize the social implications of Thérèse's teachings: "The significance of the little things we leave undone! The protests we do not make, the stands we do not take, we who are living in the world." But she was also taken by Thérèse's convictions that we all are called to be saints and that all holiness is rooted in the practice of love.

For Day, the practical wisdom of Thérèse's "science of love" was amply confirmed by her own experience of community life among the "insulted and injured." The Catholic Worker still has no rules or tests for inclusion; all are welcome. The result is an assembly of characters seemingly drawn from a novel by Dostoevsky: an array of pilgrims, scholars, and "holy fools," young and old, workers, wastrels, the crazed, the unwashed, and the unwanted. Only love could preserve such a household.

Yet Day was not blind to the tensions and difficulties involved. In one of her journals, after describing the various types of irritating people—demanding, ungrateful, and selfish—she noted how at times "the burden gets too heavy; there are too many of them; my love is too small; I even feel with terror, 'I have no love in my heart; I have nothing to give them'; and yet I have to pretend I have. But strange and wonderful, the make-believe becomes true. If you will to love someone you soon do. You will to love this cranky old man, and someday you do. It depends on how hard you try." It is a striking statement, an instructive answer to the common dodge: "Dorothy Day could do these things; she was a saint." Apparently if Dorothy Day could love so many apparently unlovable people, it was simply because she tried harder.

The functional anarchy of a Catholic Worker house may seem miles away from the order and regulation of a typical convent or monastery. Yet they present similar challenges, as Dorothy Day came to appreciate. Each can serve as a "school of charity." The point is not that life in community naturally fosters cooperation and understanding; quite the opposite is the case. This was precisely St. Thérèse's insight: It is easier to love people in the abstract than to tolerate the person at your table, the one who makes funny noises when she eats or who scrapes his knife on the plate in an annoying way. It is such trials that refine our capacity for love. For we learn forgiveness only when there is something to forgive; we learn patience when our patience is sorely tested.

Thomas Merton called the monastic community "a school where we learn to be happy." This was not because a monastery (as the sign at Disneyland proclaims) is "The Happiest Place on Earth." According to Merton, in the monastic community we learn that our happiness "consists in sharing the happiness of God." Otherwise we might be tempted to believe that our happiness consists in being rid of the idiots who surround us.

What is said of the monastic community is just as true of any family—perhaps more so, inasmuch as the family is one community that we cannot choose. Sometimes the family is a place of natural love and support, the one place where we are valued and find unconditional acceptance. At other times it can be a suffocating enclosure, if not a vipers' nest. As Tolstoy famously observed, "Happy families are all alike." But even in the "happiest" families the occasional eruption of dinner table disputes and simmering rivalries can leave one fantasizing about St. Simeon Stylites and his uncrowded life atop a pillar.

Yet this too is a school of charity. In a family, among those we know most intimately and who know us in return, we are not simply tolerated but challenged to be our better selves—more forgiving, more patient. Regardless of the quality of our family lives, we need not go in quest of such challenges. They seek us out on a daily, if not hourly, basis.

Many times Dorothy Day wept over the failings and dissensions among her Catholic Worker family, only to be consoled by some gesture of kindness or fellowship that seemed like a preview of heaven. The title of her autobiography, *The Long Loneliness*, referred to the essential solitude at the heart of any vocation. But she ended her book with these words: "We cannot love God unless we love each other. We know Him in the breaking of bread and we know each other in the breaking of bread, and we are not alone anymore. . . . We have all known the long loneliness and we have learned that the only solution is love and that love comes with community."

NEW EYES

Love allows us to see with new eyes, to look beneath appearances to a deeper truth or value. Something may be shabby and worn, lacking in evident value or quality. Yet its association with a person we love or a time when we were especially happy endows it with immeasurable worth: a child's shoe or her clumsy drawing; our father's sweater; our mother's teacup. Everything has its own secret life. Love gathers these disparate objects and makes them channels of grace. For the saints the whole natural order, loved by God and therefore infinitely precious, bears this potential. Insofar as we participate in this love, all things disclose their transcendent meaning; each of them calls us to our true home.

We know that we are surrounded at all times by forces that remain invisible to our unassisted eyes: ultraviolet rays from the sun, electromagnetic waves, radio signals or television images, the conversations that bounce between cellular phones. If some tincture could render these waves and forces visible, we would find ourselves swimming in a sea of light, color, and sound, all dimensions of a reality that forms no part of our normal perception or consciousness.

The saints were attuned to a similar invisible reality: the fact that we all are connected in a web of love and that the universe is rooted and sustained in a reality that, if we had eyes to see, would at once astonish and awaken us from the dream of separateness.

Awakened by these "beams of love," a young Catholic priest named Engelmar Unzeitig found the meaning of his vocation in the midst of a Nazi concentration camp in Bavaria. Among the two hundred thousand inmates of Dachau, Unzeitig was one of the more than twenty-five hundred Christian clergy. These prisoners were held in particular contempt by their Nazi captors, who segregated the clergy from the rest of the population in their own special barracks. Amid the filth and horror of the camp, these priests and pastors lived out their ministry. They prayed together, Catholics with Protestants. They composed hymns, celebrated clandestine masses, and otherwise tried to serve their fellow prisoners. With good reason, Dachau was called "the largest monastery in the world."

For Father Engelmar, who had been arrested in Austria soon after his ordination for preaching in defense of the Jews, Dachau was virtually his first "assignment" as a priest.

He tried to regard it as a school for holiness. In a letter smuggled out to his sister, he wrote: "What sometimes appears as misfortune is often the greatest fortune. How much a person learns only through experience in the school of life. We should feel and experience for others, I think, the lack of peace in the world and help them to true peace. Then we are not surprised if God takes from us some things which are dear and precious to us."

In December 1944 the camp was hit with a terrible outbreak of typhoid. More than two thousand prisoners died in the first month. To stem the epidemic, infected prisoners were confined to a squalid barracks, where they were essentially left to die, alone and uncared for. Within the hell of Dachau this was surely the inner sanctum. Nevertheless, when a call went out for volunteer orderlies, twenty priests stepped forward. Father Engelmar was among them. Given the extremely infectious nature of the disease, the meaning of this gesture was clear to all; there was little hope that any volunteers would survive. Yet into this void the priests brought their love and faith, doing what they could to bring some consolation and dignity to the place. Simply caring for the sick and keeping them clean provided endless work. But the priests also heard confessions, offered last rites, and recited the prayers for the dead. Because the SS would not enter this barracks, it afforded its own peculiar zone of humanity.

Within weeks Father Engelmar was burning with fever. He died on March 2, 1945, the day after his thirty-fourth birthday and only a few weeks before the liberation of the camp by U.S. troops. In a letter written just days before his death, he said: "The Good is undying and victory must remain with God, even if it sometimes seems useless for us to spread love in the world. Nevertheless, one sees again and again that *the human heart is attuned to love, and it cannot withstand its power in the long run, if it is truly based on God and not on creatures.* We want to continue to do and offer everything so that love and peace may soon reign again."

Six

LEARNING TO SUFFER

For the saint, suffering continues to be suffering, but it ceases to be an obstacle to his mission, or to his happiness, both of which are found positively and concretely in the will of God. —Thomas Merton

IT MAY SEEM FOOLISH to speak of suffering in connection with the pursuit of happiness. "No pain, no gain," the saying goes, but that applies to dieting and exercise. Real pain is something else. Surely happiness—whatever the word implies—requires the greatest possible distance between ourselves and everything that hurts. Were it otherwise, we might be inclined to "pass." Yet suffering will come to us all the same.

It is not astonishing to learn that we can find happiness through work, through love, through inner peace, or detachment from everyday cares. Each of these pursuits, after all, implies a certain contentment. But to say that we shall be happy if only we learn to be content is a mere tautology. Our contentment is thin fare if it can be undone by a flea, a spark, a patch of ice, a broken twig. And so it is here that we most need the guidance of the saints. For they have known a path to happiness on which suffering is no necessary impediment.

One approaches this lesson with humility. Suffering is cold, hard, and repellent, and only those who have suffered can speak with assurance and without risk of seeming glib. St. John the Evangelist restricted his testimony to "what we have seen and heard," and there is particular peril, in this case, in talking about what one does not know firsthand. Yet the subject cannot be avoided. What, after all, is the value of any prescription for happiness if it depends ultimately on happy circumstances beyond our control?

The saints do not teach us how to avoid suffering; they teach us how to suffer. They do not provide the "meaning" of suffering. But they lived by the assurance that there is a meaning or truth at the heart of life that suffering is powerless to destroy. They did not believe that suffering is "good" but that God is good and that "neither death nor life . . . nor height, nor depth" can deprive us of access to that good if we truly desire it. They found that there is no place that is literally "godforsaken," but that in every situation, even the most grim and painful, there is a door that leads to love, to fullness of life . . . to happiness. This is the deepest mystery of the gospel. Our task, if we would learn from the saints, is to find that door and enter in.

THE CENTER OF THE WHEEL

Some saints have written whole treatises on suffering. The first of these was by St. Severinus Boethius (480–524), author of *The Consolation of Philosophy*. His work, which was inspired by his own experience of misfortune, deals explicitly with the relationship between suffering and happiness. Boethius was a wellborn Christian who served as a high official in the Roman court. When he became embroiled in a palace intrigue, he was charged with treason as well as "the impious study of philosophy." Stripped of his honors, he was imprisoned, tortured, and eventually executed. In prison, he composed his book, written in the form of a dialogue with his personified patron, Philosophia. Comforting her disciple in his sufferings, "Lady Philosophy" urges Boethius to become detached from worldly cares and to focus instead on the only supreme good, God, the Creator of all things. If he can achieve such an attitude, his peace and equilibrium will no longer depend on outward circumstances.

Among Boethius's lasting legacies is his depiction of life as a slowly turning wheel of fortune, a classical image that here received a Christian appropriation. According to Boethius, those who enjoy wealth, power, fame, and the like are literally "on the rise." But Fortune's wheel continues to turn, so it is foolish to seek happiness in things that are passing—truly here today and gone tomorrow. As long as we cling to the surface of the wheel, we are never satisfied. "It takes very little to spoil the perfect happiness of the fortunate," Lady Philosophy observes. So it is in our own lives. Our prosperity and contentment are shadowed by care and anxiety. We have only to compare ourselves with our neighbors to find something lacking: "The joy of human happiness is shot through with bitterness; no matter how pleasant it seems when one has it, such happiness cannot be kept when it decides to leave."

What solution does Philosophia propose? If we would be

happy, she advises, we must leave the wheel's outer rim, the illusion that happiness can be found in transitory goods. We must move Godward—that is, toward the center of the wheel, which never changes. In that case, it follows that the way to happiness is indeed inseparably linked to the pursuit of holiness. But what is holiness, according to Boethius? Is it just another name for stoic resignation? The answer depends on what we find at the center of the wheel. On that subject, philosophy alone takes us only so far.

Later in the Middle Ages Meister Eckhart assumed a more pragmatic approach to suffering. In *The Book of Divine Comfort*, written in the early fourteenth century, Eckhart proposes "some thirty arguments, any one of which should be sufficient to comfort an honest person in his distress." Some of Eckhart's points are pitched rather high, indeed over the heads of everyone but a fellow mystic: "A really perfect person will be so dead to self, so lost in God, so given over to the will of God, that his whole happiness consists in being unconscious of self and its concerns . . . and wishing to know nothing except the will of and truth of God." At other times he comes closer to earth, offering a type of medieval "chicken soup for the soul." Take, for example, his reflection on the maxim "There is no loss that is pure loss." Eckhart describes a man who has a hundred dollars and loses forty. The more he thinks of the forty dollars he lost, the more anguished he will be, especially "if he keeps visualizing it, brooding over it, his eyes heavy with sorrow, talking to his loss and the loss persuading him as if they two were persons staring into each other's faces." But as Eckhart points out, the man still has sixty dollars left, and if he only concentrated on that, he would surely find some consolation. He might, for that matter, "stop growling" and give thanks that he had a hundred dollars in the first place!

At times Eckhart's advice brings to mind the homely platitudes of barbershop wisdom: "If you would be comforted, forget those who have it better off and think of those worse off." (In other words, "Count your blessings!") Or this: A man traveling by a certain road falls down and breaks his leg. He is likely to think, "If only I had traveled by another road!" But how much better to think: "Still greater harm might have befallen me if I had taken the other road." (Translation: "It could be worse!") At other points Eckhart's arguments recall the counsel of Philosophia to Boethius: Our suffering comes from "living on the outside of things, far away from God and not being empty or innocent of creatures, not being like God." (True enough, though some might find it cold comfort, in their suffering, to be told, in effect, "Cheer up! Be more like God!")

No doubt there is wisdom in many of these arguments. When we are detached from our sufferings, or compare them with the misfortunes of others, or weigh them against our blessings, we may indeed achieve a wider perspective. And there is no telling the effect of even the most familiar cliché delivered at the right moment. Once, after Dorothy Day gave a lecture, a man in the audience thanked her profusely, claiming that her talk had changed his life. When she asked him what in particular had impressed him, he answered, "I think it was where you said, 'It's never too late to turn over a new leaf.' "

Nevertheless, in the end, it is the rare sufferer who finds adequate consolation in philosophical arguments, regardless of their source or ingenuity. In fact, most of us would gladly exchange a whole book of arguments for one act of kindness from a friend who reached out to share our burden.

The experience of suffering can make us feel that an indifferent universe is arrayed against us. Even the most steadfast atheists take solace in finding that they are not alone, that there is even one person who cares and understands their secret sorrows and who responds with compassion. The word "compassion" itself means "to suffer with." And perhaps Eckhart is on his strongest ground when he invokes no longer the plight of those who have it worse, but instead the boundless compassion of God.

After all, the God revealed in Jesus did not sit impassively on the sidelines, unaffected by the world's suffering. Christ's path led him to the cross, the point where suffering was geometrically concentrated. When the cross becomes an image of the still axis of the turning world, it means that our sorrows and suffering do not fall on indifferent ears but correspond to a principle of mercy and compassion at the very heart of reality. Thus Eckhart takes us beyond the consolation of philosophy. "Since God is with us when we suffer, he suffers with us," Eckhart explains. And if, as we know, misery is diminished by the sympathy of a friend, "how much more shall I find comfort in the compassion of God."

LIVES OF THE SAINTS

Not every saint has written a treatise on suffering. But there is scarcely one of them whose life was not significantly marked by its reality, whether by persecution, sickness, hunger, or privation; the death of friends and family; the failure of grand projects and private dreams; the exhaustion of fruitless labors or hopes stillborn; loneliness; the spiritual torment of acedia or what St. John of the Cross called "the dark night of the soul." One could easily tell their stories as a chronicle of pain.

St. Paul positively boasted of his sufferings: "We rejoice that we have been counted worthy to suffer," he exclaimed. "Five times I have received the forty lashes less one. Three times I have been beaten with rods; once I was stoned. Three times I have been shipwrecked; a night and a day I have been adrift at sea; on frequent journeys in danger from rivers, danger from robbers, dangers from my own people, danger from Gentiles, danger in the city, danger in the wilderness, danger at sea, danger from false brethren; in toil and hardship, through many a sleepless night, in hunger and thirst, often without food, in cold and exposure . . ." (2 Cor. 11:24–27).

If in some cases suffering was simply the price of discipleship, in others it was the crucible in which faith was refined and tested. And in not a few cases suffering played a crucial role in a saint's conversion or the discernment of a vocation.

The first biography of St. Francis of Assisi, for example, begins with a description of his early life as a carefree, indeed prodigal youth who "squandered and wasted his life miserably" and "outdid his contemporaries in vanities, pomp, and vainglory." The turning point in his life came with a prolonged illness, after his return from war, which gave him time "to think of things other than he was used to thinking upon." When he recovered somewhat and could walk with the support of a cane, "he went outside one day and began to look about at the surrounding landscape with great interest." As his biographer, Thomas of Celano, observed, "From that day on . . . he began to despise himself and to hold in some contempt the things he had admired and loved before." There were other steps leading to Francis's joyous leap into poverty. But what is notable in his story is how suffering offered a new vantage point, allowing him to view the world with new "interest," while at the same time throwing a harsh light on the "vanity" of his previous existence.

Suffering played a similar role for St. Ignatius of Loyola (1491–1556), the Basque founder of the Jesuit order. In his autobiography (written in the third person), he described himself, until the age of twenty-six, as a man "given over to the vanities of the world." A soldier and courtier, he "delighted especially in the exercise of arms." This delight nearly ended his life when, during a heated battle, his leg was shattered by a French cannonball. Though he survived the initial injury, his leg was set so badly that it had to be broken and set again. He endured this treatment, by his own account, without speaking a word, "nor showed any sign of pain other than to clench his fists." But by the time his leg was mended he was upset that an unsightly bulge in his knee disrupted the handsome line of his figure. "Determined to make himself a martyr to his own pleasure," he insisted on having his leg cut and reset again, "although the pain was greater than all those he had suffered."

During his long convalescence Ignatius asked for something to read, preferably stories of courtly adventure. Instead he was given a book of lives of the saints. At first he read only to relieve his boredom. But gradually he became absorbed by these tales of spiritual valor, so different from his previous concepts of honor and courage. Soon he found himself pondering: "What if I should do what St. Francis did, what St. Dominic did?" These fancies "alternated with thoughts of wordly adventures." And yet, he said, there was a difference. "When he was thinking about the things of the world, he took much delight in them, but afterward, when he was tired and put them aside, he found that he was dry and discontented. But when he thought of going to Jerusalem, barefoot and eating nothing but herbs and undergoing all the other rigors that he saw the saints had endured, not only was he consoled when he had these thoughts, but even after putting them aside, he remained content and happy." The result is that by the time he fully recovered he was no longer the same man, no longer defined by the same ambitions. He had given himself over to the cause of Christ.

Among the saints there are many similar stories that illustrate the capacity of suffering or misfortune to disrupt the force of inertia in our lives, thus releasing energies now available for a new purpose or goal. In one case it might be illness, in another the loss of loved ones, or the collapse of some ambition, that causes us to reflect on what is at stake in life and leads us on a quest for deeper answers. We are no longer satisfied to live on the surface of the wheel.

A SPIRITUAL GUIDE

If suffering accomplished no more than to expose the hollowness or "vanity" of our lives the result might well be despair. But in the lives of the saints, suffering accomplished something more. It did not simply strip away their illusions but also opened new possibilities and quickened their sensitivity to the presence of grace. Suffering, in this sense, could be a merciful friend and a profound spiritual guide. Recognizing this paradoxical truth, some saints have even prayed for an experience that would thrust them into the presence of the cross. Their goal was not suffering itself, but something else—insight, compassion, a state of devotional intensity—which extreme circumstances might facilitate.

The story of Julian of Norwich (1342–1416), an English recluse and mystic, is a notable example. In her *Revelations of Divine Love* (or *Showings*) she described how, in her youth, she prayed that she might experience a grave illness to the point of death, that she might receive direct knowledge of Christ's passion, and that she might receive the "three wounds" of contrition, compassion, and longing for God.

In any time such a prayer might seem morbidly presumptuous. To a modern audience, determined to avoid pain at any cost, Julian's prayer may appear utterly incomprehensible. It is worth noting that Julian was a survivor of the Black Death. She lived in a time when suffering was as real and pervasive as the hunger for its meaning. Julian undertook to experience suffering so that she might truly understand its nature and find its meaning in a personal experience of Christ's passion. In her own words, her aim was "to be purged by God's mercy, and afterwards live more to his glory because of that sickness."

Julian believed her prayer was answered at the age of thirty when she developed a mysterious and devastating illness. For four days and nights she hovered in a state of paralysis and excruciating pain. When at last a priest was summoned to administer the last rites, he held a cross before her frozen gaze. Suddenly all pain and distress left her. At that moment, according to her account, she saw Jesus in the flesh, and a flesh in pain. He spoke to her and gave a vivid account of his physical sufferings as well as other holy mysteries. It was in one of these memorable visions that she saw the world as if it were a hazelnut in the hand of God and grew confident that ultimately, no matter what happened to us in the flesh, "all shall be well, and all shall be well, and all manner of things shall be well."

Julian's vision of Christ's suffering was clinically graphic: "I saw the red blood running down from under the crown, hot and flowing freely and copiously, a living stream. . . . The great drops of blood fell . . . like a herring's scales." She saw his skin broken by scourging; the "sweet flesh," parched by thirst, "drying before my eyes." Yet for all the pain of watching this suffering, her contemplation turned toward the depths of love, knowing "why and for whom" he suffered. This became for Julian a source of consolation and rejoicing. As she watched the death of Christ, "Suddenly he changed to an appearance of joy—the reason why he suffers is because in his goodness he wishes to make us heirs with him of his joy." In one of her "showings" Christ disclosed his meaning: "Are you well satisfied that I suffered for you? . . . If you are satisfied, I am satisfied. It is a joy, a bliss, an endless delight to me that ever I suffered my Passion for you; and if I could suffer more I should suffer more. . . ."

When Julian, against all expectations, did not die but rather recovered completely, she wrote down all the revelations that had been given her—not in clerical Latin but in vernacular Middle English—and eventually retired to an anchor-hold attached to the Church of St. Julian and St. Hugh, in which she intended to spend her days reflecting on the extraordinary insight she had received, not only into the suffering of Jesus but into its meaning.

So renowned was the anchoress Julian (she took her name from the church in Norwich where she resided; we do not know her real name) that she daily received at the grated window of her cell visitors desperate for the wisdom of one who had suffered firsthand with the ultimate model of suffering and who had not been defeated but had emerged enlarged and energized by it.

How might Julian's visions from the fourteenth century speak to our own sufferings? Her mystical view of Christ's passion reflected a traditional understanding, according to which Jesus, by his suffering on the cross, "paid" the debt for human sin. Many no longer find this language comforting or even plausible. But Julian's vision extended beyond such penal imagery. For her the depth of Jesus' suffering showed the depth of God's compassion—God's willingness to *suffer with us*. While some might take comfort in God's inscrutable wisdom, Julian stressed the immensity of God's love. She saw that suffering did not have the last word, and so she gained an insight into the divine truth that we are all "soul and body, clad and enclosed in the goodness of God." This—neither despair nor stoic resignation—was the insight that Julian won by means of her suffering.

It requires little imagination to take a further step, to regard our own sufferings as an exercise in compassion—in this case an opportunity to *suffer with God*—and therefore also an expression of love. It takes little imagination but much love. So the saints teach us.

PASSIVE DIMINISHMENT

We use only a small portion of our brain. There are muscles in our body that atrophy for lack of exercise. And there are, similarly, portions of our humanity that remain dormant and undiscovered until certain experiences come along—like falling in love, having a child, or facing death—that bring them to life. Suffering is surely one of these experiences. Léon Bloy, the French Catholic novelist, wrote, "In his poor heart man has places which do not yet exist and into them enters suffering in order to bring them to life."

Are they worth the price—these not-yet-existent places in the heart? We all know that suffering does not necessarily make us holy or even nice. It is just as likely to foster bitterness, self-pity, and cynicism. It is a serious error to imagine that suffering in itself is ever "good." But it can be productive. If our definition of happiness requires the absolute avoidance of suffering, then any pain or frustration is an obstacle to our goal. But the saints saw their goal differently. Most of them would have endorsed the words of St. Ignatius in his *Spiritual Exercises*, that human beings are "created to praise, reverence, and serve God" and by this means to attain eternal life. To the extent that we fulfill this mission we achieve our happiness. And toward this goal, it so happens, suffering is no impediment. It may even be an ally.

Friedrich Nietzsche wrote, "What does not destroy me makes me stronger." The saints, for their part, did not prize strength as much as compassion. As a plow breaks open hardened soil so that it can receive more water, so suffering can break open hardened hearts and make them receptive to deeper wisdom. In the words of Diadochos of Photiki, one of the early desert fathers, "As wax cannot take the imprint of a seal unless it is warmed or softened thoroughly, so a man cannot receive the seal of God's holiness unless he is tested by labors and weaknesses." St. Teresa called suffering "the Royal Way of the Cross," the way that was traveled and prepared by Christ the King. In that light, what does not destroy us may make us better able to bear God's image.

Pierre Teilhard de Chardin, a French Jesuit and mystic, wrote about the constructive impact of suffering and failure: "The lives of the saints and, generally speaking, the lives of all those who have been outstanding for intelligence or goodness are full of these instances in which one can see the person emerging ennobled, tempered, and renewed from some ordeal, or even some downfall, which seemed bound to diminish or lay him low forever. Failure in that case plays for us the part that the elevator plays for an aircraft or the pruning knife for a plant. It canalizes the sap of our inward life, disengages the purest 'components' of our being in such a way as to make us shoot up higher and straighter."

As a theologian and paleontologist, Teilhard sought to reconcile the cosmic mysticism of St. Paul with the insights of evolution and contemporary cosmology. He spent many years exploring the Gobi Desert in China, collecting rocks and the fossilized artifacts of human origins. His scientific imagination led him to see life and the universe in the widest possible perspective: the explosion of stars, the violent formation of great landmasses, and the tectonic shifts that resulted in mountains and canyons. But with the eyes of faith he also discerned in the evolutionary process a guiding principle behind the transition from inanimate matter to primitive and ever more complex forms of life. These organisms in turn evolve in the direction of consciousness, love, and higher forms of spiritual energy.

Teilhard believed it is possible to discern a similar process in the life of individuals, a principle of humanization that enables us to achieve our highest spiritual potential—in other words, to become holy. In this process we are formed not only by our conscious choices but also, and perhaps to a greater extent, by what we undergo involuntarily. He called this the principle of passive diminishment. It includes all the bits of ill fortune in our lives: "the barrier which blocks our way, the wall that hems us in, the invisible microbe that invades our body, the little word that infects the mind . . . all the incidents and accidents of varying importance and varying kinds, the tragic interferences . . . which come between the world of 'other' things and the world that radiates out from us." But it also includes the passage of time, the gradual deterioration of old age, "little by little robbing us of ourselves and pushing us on toward the end." Teilhard believed that we are shaped and measured by our defeats as well as by our achievements; by our weaknesses as well as our strengths; by what we do and by what we endure. Both joy and suffering unleash spiritual energies that connect us to the divine center of reality.

Teilhard himself knew both achievement and endurance. The church authorities of his time were suspicious of his efforts to reconcile Christian theology and evolutionary science. They accused him of undermining the doctrine of original sin and the biblical account of creation. Forbidden to lecture publicly or publish any of his theological speculations, he worked under a constant cloud of reproval and aspersions on his orthodoxy. These restrictions caused him great suffering and contributed, no doubt, to his insights on passive diminishment. Only after his death in 1955 were his writings published. They generated phenomenal interest, a stark contrast with the obscurity of his lifelong labors.

Among those touched by Teilhard's vision was Flannery O'Connor, a young Catholic writer living in Georgia, who described the subject of all her stories as being "the action of grace on a character who is not very willing to support it." In her fiction O'Connor frequently depicted characters who were stopped short, stripped of their illusions—whether of bourgeois virtue, social status, smug rationalism, or quiet good taste—so that they might receive a deeper truth about their own sins and their need for forgiveness. A self-described "hillbilly Thomist," O'Connor felt keenly the challenge of writing about such realities as the incarnation, original sin, and redemption for an audience to whom these words were meaningless "idiocies." Often, in writing to correspondents who doubted that Catholic faith could be reconciled with human intelligence, she recommended Teilhard's writings by way of rebuttal. But out of all of Teilhard's work it appears that the concept of passive diminishment struck a particularly personal chord.

Early in O'Connor's life she was diagnosed with lupus, the same degenerative disease that had killed her father. For her survival she depended on regular cortisone shots that gradually dissolved her joints and made it difficult to walk without crutches. Her condition confined her to her family's dairy farm outside Milledgeville, Georgia, where she wrote as her strength permitted—two hours in the morning—and otherwise tended the menagerie of ducks, swans, and peafowl with which she surrounded herself.

O'Connor possessed a sharp ear for the absurd and a capacity to reconcile what she called the comic and the terrible. She disliked sentimental piety and reacted strongly against the temptation of critics to drag her medical history into a consideration of her work. Yet her illness imposed a discipline and sense of priorities that she managed to turn to the advantage of her art. In her letters she appropriated Teilhard's phrase "passive diminishment" to describe a quality she admired, the serene acceptance of whatever affliction or loss no effort was likely to change. "I have enough energy to write with," she said, "and as that is all I have any business doing anyhow, I can with one eye squinted take it all as a blessing. What you have to measure out, you come to observe closer."

Although the Catholic framework of her writing was widely recognized, it was the posthumous publication of O'Connor's letters that best revealed her own character and the deep correspondence between her artistic "message" and her own spiritual voice. She believed that her highest responsibility as an artist was to the good of her art. But as a Christian she also regarded her own life as a work in progress. The meaning of such a life is not measured in outward success. Our highest responsibility as human beings—again, in Ignatius's phrase—is "to praise, reverence, and serve God," employing the relative gifts we possess in the circumstances that are given us. As O'Connor noted, "The creative action of the Christian's life is to prepare his death in Christ. It is a continuous action in which this world's goods are utilized to the fullest, both positive gifts and what Père Teilhard de Chardin calls 'passive diminishments.' "

There is no doubt that O'Connor "utilized" these "goods"—both her positive talents and her sufferings—as she made her way toward what she called her "true country." As she wrote to a friend, "I have never been anywhere but sick. In a sense sickness is a place, more instructive than a long trip to Europe, and it's always a place where there's no company, where nobody can follow."

O'Connor died at age thirty-nine. Her short life was lacking in external drama ("Lives spent between the house and the chicken yard do not make exciting copy"). But while she was restricted in her mobility, it is hard to think that hers was an impoverished life. She was no mystic in the usual sense, yet she lived deeply from the standpoint of what she called the central Christian mystery, the same insight that Julian of Norwich received in her divine "showings": that this world has, "for all its horrors, been found by God to be worth dying for."

THE WILL OF GOD

Among Meister Eckhart's "guaranteed" consolations is the following. Suffering does me no harm, he says, "if I accept the suffering and transfigure the pain into the will of God." Under this condition, "I shall be even-tempered, wholly comfortable and happy, under all circumstances."

Preachers throughout history have urged such counsel on the poor and wretched of the earth. Whether or not it has increased the balance of human happiness is hard to say. In the absence of alternatives, it may be consoling, when we are faced by earthquakes, droughts, and plagues, to invoke "the will of God." Confronting the starvation of a child, or the persistence of poverty, or the suffering of a loved one with AIDS, we may find strength to endure if we "transfigure the pain into the will of God." Or we may come to despise God.

There is an alternative, however, to vulgar resignation. We have previously considered the work of Jean-Pierre de Caussade, whose *Abandonment to Divine Providence* enjoins us to seek God's will in the present moment. Caussade points to the spiritual dimension of all our daily activities: the tasks and duties we must perform; our encounters with other people. Each one of these is a "sacrament" that carries the will of God for us in that moment. To live in such a state of mindfulness is to be alive to the sacred depths of our everyday experience.

But this discipline bears a particular challenge for us when we suffer. Simply put, it is the insight that our spiritual attitude does not depend on our outward circumstances. Even in the midst of grave misfortune there is access to God. It is precisely by faith that we can penetrate the veil of ill fortune and touch something constant and true. This accounts for the difference between those who are crushed by their circumstances and those who learn to transcend or, as Eckhart put it, "transfigure" them.

One might consider, as Caussade does, the example of the two thieves who were crucified beside Christ. Though their external circumstances were identical, their inner dispositions offered a stark contrast. Whereas one spent his dying moments on spiteful taunts, the other addressed Jesus in a spirit of trust: "Lord, remember me when you come into your kingdom." This difference meant that for the first one physical suffering was compounded by bitterness and resentment, while the other was able to transcend his condition and touch eternity. To him Jesus responded, "This day shall you be with me in Paradise."

Caussade claimed to call for nothing extraordinary, just "to carry on as you are doing and endure what you have to do—but change your attitude to all these things. And this change is simply to say 'I will' to all that God asks."

I will? The mind balks on the edge of that precipice, fearing what monsters may lie beyond. Could anyone think of directing such advice to political prisoners or the victims of terrorism? Caussade's immediate readers were the Visitation

Sisters, whom he served as a spiritual director. What, we might wonder, could such nuns know of the cruelty of life, the darkness of history? Yet it was nuns like these who in a mere generation were outlawed during the revolutionary Terror in France, stripped of their habits, and marched to the guillotine.

Still, to ascribe such suffering to the "will of God" may strike a dull note today. Where is the will of God in the Holocaust? In the sufferings of the Cambodians? In the collapse of the World Trade Center? In the bombing of Iraq? For that matter, in the suffering of a single child?

But there is another way to consider this expression. The "will of God" takes on a different meaning if it is more than simply a phrase intoned to justify bad things that happen. We may transpose these words from a conclusion into a challenge, the challenge to seek God's presence under the disguise of every circumstance. In other words, the "will of God" need not serve as a benediction over our fate; God does not "will" that we suffer. It is, instead, the latent challenge that meets us within, or despite, every situation, the challenge to respond in a way that bears witness to love, to justice, to the truth.

Sheila Cassidy, an English physician, discovered this challenge under the most difficult conditions. Working as a doctor in Chile in the early 1970s, she was swept up in the wave of violent repression that followed a military coup. Despite her lack of political engagement, she was arrested for treating a wounded revolutionary. Along with many thousands of others she was tortured and interned in a prison camp. Many of these detainees simply disappeared. In Cassidy's case, international pressure finally secured her release and her expulsion from the country. In her memoir *Audacity to*

Believe, Cassidy described the power of torture to turn her into a ragged ball of fear and pain. Those who have experienced this trauma are permanently marked, not simply by the memory of total pain but by the knowledge of what human beings can do to one another.

She wrote that after the torture stopped and she had a bit of emotional space to maneuver, her first instinct was to scream out to God for help, "to batter spiritually on the bars of my cage, begging to be released." Then a curious idea came to her. Perhaps it was better "to hold out my empty hands to God, not in supplication but in offering. I would say, not 'Please let me out' but, 'Here I am Lord, take me. I trust you. Do with me what you will. . . .' In my powerlessness and captivity there remained to me one freedom: I could abandon myself into the hands of God."

The effect of this prayer was not an instant transformation in her attitude but a gradual process in which she found the necessary courage and strength to meet the occasion. As she said, "This option for abandonment is available to all who find themselves trapped by circumstance and is the means by which the imprisoned can transcend their bonds. Like a bird in a cage they can choose to exhaust themselves battering their wings against the bars—or they can learn to live within the confines of their prison and find, to their surprise, that they have the strength to sing."

The situation of a political prisoner may be exceptional. But later, as a hospice doctor in England, Cassidy found that her experience in Chile gave her some common ground with her terminally ill cancer patients. She could understand their desperate questions: "Why me? What have I done to deserve this?" She also found that insights drawn from her own encounter with suffering might apply to any persons in desperate circumstances that they are powerless to alter. We can spend our energy in bitterness and despair, "battering our wings" against the cage, or we can join our prayer to that of Mary—"Behold the handmaiden of the Lord. Let it be done unto me according to your will"—and discover that we have "the strength to sing." It is a prayer that can be uttered with confidence that God's will for us is not obliteration but that we may this day be with him—which is to say, in paradise.

An American Jesuit priest, Walter Ciszek, discovered a similar freedom and serenity during his years as a prisoner in the Soviet gulag. Father Ciszek was serving in a mission in eastern Poland at the beginning of World War II when Soviet troops invaded. Not wanting to be separated from his flock, Ciszek willingly accompanied Polish workers being deported to Russia for forced labor. When his priestly identity was discovered, he was arrested as a spy. He spent five years in solitary confinement in the Lubyanka Prison in Moscow before being sentenced to fifteen years of hard labor. He served the entire sentence, plus another three years of exile in Siberia, before he was abruptly shipped back to the United States in 1963.

During his twenty-three years of confinement Ciszek faced death on many occasions; the cruelty and hardship of his experience can hardly be described. Yet he said that his greatest suffering came when he mentally fought against the injustice of his fate. To the extent that he abandoned himself to Providence, convinced that in every situation he was exactly where God wanted him to be, he felt a sense of freedom and peace. His ordeals took on meaning—whether in the spiritual comfort he could offer his fellow prisoners, or in the witness of his priestly ministry, or simply, in some mysterious way, in his identification with the suffering of

Christ. At such times he experienced a "feeling of joy, that confidence in the simple and direct faith expressed in trusting [God] alone."

Father Ciszek later wrote that it is a great temptation, when things do not turn out the way we planned, to become disappointed and want to run away: "This life is not what I thought it would be. This is not what I bargained for. . . . You must forgive me, God, but I want to go back." He too knew this temptation. But his consolation was always to return in trust to the "will of God": "Not the will of God as we might wish it, or as we might have envisioned it, or as we thought in our poor human wisdom it ought to be. But rather the will of God as God envisioned it and revealed it to us each day in the created situations with which he presented us. His will for us was the twenty-four hours of each day: the people, the places, the circumstances he set before us in that time. Those were the things God knew were important to him and to us *at that moment*, and those were the things upon which he wanted us to act. . . ."

During his time in solitary confinement in Lubyanka Father Ciszek found the strength to "let go," to turn the reins of his life over to God. He was a priest with a vocation to bear the image of Christ in the world. He could be a priest in prison as well as in a parish. For his fellow prisoners he could strive to be an image of mercy and forgiveness, a reminder in the midst of the Soviet system of the spiritual dimension of existence. It was never easy, but it was not impossible. God was asking him "to see these suffering men around me, these circumstances in the prison, as sent from his hand and ordained by his providence."

Echoes of Jean-Pierre de Caussade abound in Father Ciszek's memoirs, and his testimony adds vivid credibility to what might otherwise be dismissed as pious idealism: "God is in all things, sustains all things, directs all things. To discern this in every situation and circumstance, to see his will in all things, was to accept each circumstance and situation and let oneself be borne along in perfect confidence and trust. Nothing could separate me from him, because he was in all things."

In writing of his ordeal, Father Ciszek displayed no trace of bitterness or regrets. Though his experience was unusual, to say the least, he believed its lessons could apply to people in every situation. "For each of us, salvation means no more and no less than taking up daily the same cross of Christ, accepting each day what it brings as the will of God, offering back to God each morning all the joys, works, and sufferings of that day." He discovered that it was possible to be happy even in a prison cell, even in a Siberian labor camp. The secret was simply to live each moment with a sense of purpose and responsibility, determined to find in each situation and each person he encountered the way to God. He did not seek in vain: "No one can know greater peace, no one can be more committed, no one can achieve a greater sense of fulfillment in his life than the person who believes in this truth of the faith and strives daily to put it into practice. If it all seems too simple, you have only to try it to find how difficult it is. But you have only to try it to find out as well the joy and the peace and the happiness it can bring."

READING OUR STORY

It is one thing to seek the way of holiness and happiness that lies in the present moment. But our lives are more than a succession of present moments. There is also a narrative arc to our experience, a story that can be told about our lives. It may be a story marked by suffering, but suffering is not the subject of the story. This insight may go some way toward answering the inevitable question: What is the meaning of my suffering? Perhaps we take too narrow a view. We ought, instead, to seek the meaning of our lives.

It is difficult to survey our lives as a whole if we confine our search to "the present moment." In the midst of anguish we may perceive nothing but a void, a sense of utter loneliness. When we suffer, we are prone to think that God has abandoned us. If he had been doing his job, we would not be suffering now. Such is the rebuke that Mary of Bethany, the sister of Lazarus, directed to Jesus: "If you had been here, sir, my brother would not have died . . ." (John 11:32). But if I see my life as an ongoing story, believing that on some level it is also God's story, then I know that its meaning is not to be found in one moment or another—neither in the best nor in the worst moment—but in the shape of the story itself. Lazarus did die, but he was not abandoned by God, and his death was not the final word.

St. Augustine was perhaps the first to look at his life in this way—not as a succession of discrete episodes but as a text to be plumbed and examined as the material for spiritual reflection. He surveyed his past from the standpoint of his conversion, the great pivotal point in his life. In this light he could discern God's providential hand, caring for him and guiding him toward his eventual happiness, even in those times of moral and psychological floundering when the thought of God was far from him: "You were guiding me as a helmsman steers a ship, but the course you steered was beyond my understanding." Until his discovery of God he had sought happiness in friendship, pleasure, status, and learning. But his apparent success was continuously shadowed by sadness and suffering. Something was missing; something was lost that he could not name. Yet as he later realized, he had never been truly alone, for "all the while, far above, your mercy hovered faithfully about me."

When suffering grips us, nothing else seems to exist. The present pain, loss, or betrayal looms over us with Himalayan proportions. But we lack the perspective to see how the closing of one path may open another. What appears to be the collapse of our hopes and plans may be the occasion for new opportunity. In winter the ground appears dead. But this is only nature's temporary mask. So with faith we may learn to see that an element of apparent dying always precedes new life, that "unless a seed falls into the ground and dies it bears no fruit." In every life there are defeats and losses that appear, at least in the short term, calamitous. But the saints believed there is a providence that guides our steps, even when it leads us where we would not go.

Carlo Carretto (1910–1988) was a member of the Little Brothers of the Gospel, an order based on the spirituality of Charles de Foucauld. The Little Brothers live in small communities among the poor and forgotten of the world, thereby imitating Christ in his "hidden" years as a carpenter in Nazareth. When at the age of forty-four Carretto joined the Little Brothers, he had already spent a long public career as a leader of the Catholic youth movement in Italy. To many of his friends, his flight to the desert was an inexplicable retreat from a life of dynamic and productive service. His only explanation was that he had felt compelled to answer a call from God: "It is not your acts and deeds that I want; I want your prayer, your love." So he joined the novitiate of the Little Brothers in Algeria.

His first years in the Sahara were among the happiest in his life. The poverty, the solitude, the atmosphere of prayer— he soaked it all up. Yet Carretto nursed a secret ambition. He had always had a passion for mountaineering. He dreamed of establishing a community of Little Brothers in the Alps to help with rescue teams on the Matterhorn. It was a harmless dream. But suddenly, as if by avalanche, it was swept away. During an arduous hike in the desert he accepted a companion's offer to inject him with medicine for a minor malady. But a terrible mistake occurred. His friend picked the wrong vial and injected Carretto's thigh with a paralyzing poison. Overnight his leg became useless. He had become crippled for life.

Like anyone in these circumstances, Carretto was at first stupefied with incomprehension. Why and how could God allow such a thing to happen to his servant? "Here I came to serve him," he thought, "and all he seems to do is mock me and let me turn into a cripple."

Yet thirty years later he could describe that mistaken injection as a grace. "It was bad luck, yes. It was a misfortune. But God turned it into a grace." Unable to climb with his useless leg, he instead obtained a jeep and became a meteorologist. "Through no wish of my own, there I was where I belonged: in the desert. Instead of trudging through the snow I trudged through the sand. . . . Life suddenly appeared to me as it was, an immense personal exodus. . . . Misfortune had thrust me upon new paths."

Where is God to be found in Carretto's story? In the part of a negligent bystander who watched helplessly while an accident destroyed a man's dreams and left him crippled? Or in the grace that led Carlo Carretto from bitterness and despair to a new state of acceptance? When good comes from evil, to the eyes of faith, this is God's unmistakable signature. And so the saints' guide to happiness does not bypass the subject of suffering. As Carretto observed, "I know it by experience. You can be happy with a crippled leg. Very happy. In my experience the wounds of poverty and suffering produce a special, very precious, very sweet honey. It is the honey of the Beatitudes proclaimed by Jesus in the Sermon on the Mount. I have tasted this honey and have become convinced of the rationality of the gospel, of the reasons for so many mysterious things."

THE WHOLE CUP

To be a Christian means learning to see one's own life illuminated by the story of Jesus. In studying that story, we realize that its meaning cannot simply be reduced to a set of doctrines or ethical maxims. Nor do we find that meaning only in certain "glorious mysteries" of Jesus' life: the wedding at Cana; the multiplying of the loaves and fishes; the walking on water; or even the raising of Lazarus from the dead. It is also revealed in the pain of rejection, the betrayal and abandonment by friends, the loneliness in the garden, the anxious sweating of blood . . . the whole story.

Jesus himself realized that the joys and pains of faithfulness were inseparably mixed. On one occasion the mother of two of his disciples asked him for a favor: that in his "kingdom" one son might sit at his right side and the other on his left. Jesus replied: "You do not know what you are asking. Can you drink the cup that I am going to drink?" (Matt. 20:20–23). To drink the cup is to accept all that it contains, bitter and sweet, sorrow and glory.

This biblical text inspired one of the last books by Henri Nouwen, a Dutch priest and spiritual writer. In *Can You Drink the Cup?* he begins by meditating on the cup used at mass, remembering the particular chalice that his uncle, a bishop, gave him on the occasion of his ordination. In the course of his meditations, the cup becomes a larger symbol of life itself, the life we are called to accept, with all its contradictions. The contents are so inseparably mixed that we have no access to happiness unless we accept the whole cup. This was the lesson of Nouwen's own life.

After coming from Holland in the 1960s to study psychology in America, he taught at a series of prestigious schools: Notre Dame, Yale, Harvard. His books—more than fifty of them—won him a wide and devoted following. At the time of his death in 1996 he was one of the most popular and influential spiritual writers in the world, his popularity only enhanced by his willingness to share his own struggles and sense of brokenness. He did not present himself as a "spiritual master," but, like the title of one of his early books, as a "wounded healer."

Those who knew him were aware of how deep his wounds ran. Unlike the young Augustine, he was already a devout and committed Christian. Yet he felt a similar restlessness and anxiety about his place in the world. He was afflicted by an inordinate need for affection and affirmation; there seemed to be an inner void that could not be filled.

Nouwen had a great gift for friendship, and wherever he went he sowed the seeds of community. Still, something drove him from one place or project to another: a Trappist monastery; missions in Latin America; the idea of serving as chaplain with a traveling circus troupe. All the while the admiration of his audience only underscored a sense of isolation. With feeling he wrote about the temptations that Christ suffered in the desert: to be "relevant, powerful, and spectacular."

At this time there came a great turning point in his life. Over the years he had visited a number of L'Arche communities in France and Canada. In these communities handicapped people live together with able helpers. In 1986 he received a formal invitation from Daybreak, the L'Arche community in Toronto, to become its pastor. It was the first time in his life he had received such a formal call. With trepidation he accepted. Daybreak became his home for the rest of his life.

It was unlike anything he had ever known. Nouwen lived like other members of the community in a house with handicapped people. He was assigned to care for the most severely handicapped adult in the community, a young man named Adam, who could not talk or move by himself. Nouwen spent hours each morning bathing, dressing, and feeding Adam. Some of his old admirers wondered whether Henri Nouwen was not wasting his talents. But he found it an occasion for deep inner conversion. Adam was not impressed by Nouwen's books or his fame or his genius as a public speaker. But through this mute and helpless man, Nouwen began to know what it means to be "beloved" of God.

It was not, however, the end of his struggles. After his first year at Daybreak Nouwen suffered a nervous breakdown, doubtless the culmination of long-suppressed tensions. For months he could barely talk or leave his room.

Now he was the helpless one, mutely crying out for some affirmation of his existence. As he later described it, "Everything came crashing down—my self-esteem, my energy to live and work, my sense of being loved, my hope for healing, my trust in God . . . everything." It was an experience of total darkness, a "bottomless abyss." During those months of anguish he often wondered if God was real or just a product of his imagination.

But later he wrote, "I now know that while I felt completely abandoned, God didn't leave me alone." With the support of his friends he was able to break through and to emerge more whole, more at peace with himself. Above all, he emerged with a deeper trust in what he called "the inner voice of love," a voice calling him "beyond the boundaries of my short life, to where Christ is all in all."

Someone visiting Daybreak might be struck at first by the pain and suffering of so many members of the community. Nouwen's friend Adam had frightening seizures. Others carried heavy physical or psychological burdens. These sufferings and sorrows were realities that could not be glossed over. Yet to those who made their homes in the community it was obvious that suffering was not the only reality. There was also celebration, intimacy, and companionship, the sense of belonging and acceptance that are part of any family. It took discernment to see that joy and sorrow were intermixed—or, rather, that joys were hidden within the sorrow. As Nouwen wrote, "Somehow my life at Daybreak has given me eyes to discover joy where many others see only sorrow. . . . The sorrow is still there, but something has changed by my no longer standing in front of others but sitting with them and sharing a moment of togetherness."

When we look at Henri Nouwen's life—or at any life—in

the light of the gospel, we may ask, Where is God in this story? We have to look not only at Nouwen's achievements and glories but also at the times of his suffering and pain. They all were part of a story that ultimately bore a message of grace, the same message that Nouwen ascribed to Jesus, the fact that "real joy and peace can never be reached while bypassing suffering and death, but only by going right through them."

A FACT AND A MYSTERY

In *City of God*, St. Augustine provided a catalog of various types of suffering beginning with "the love of futile and harmful satisfactions, with its results: carping anxieties, agitations of mind, disappointments, fears, frenzied joys, quarrels, disputes, wars, treacheries, hatreds," and so forth. He went on to list "fears of disaster," every kind of loss occasioned by the "deceits and lies of men," not to mention all the dreaded calamities that have nonhuman sources ("and they are past counting"), including "the extremes of heat and cold; of storm, tempest, and flood; of thunder and lightning, hail and thunderbolt; of earthquake and upheavals; the terror of being crushed by falling buildings, of the bites of wild animals, sudden accidents. . . ." This inventory, which is hardly exhaustive, continues for several pages.

In fact, the thread of suffering runs so deeply through the fabric of our existence that were it pulled free, the remnant would unravel beyond recognition. We learn to walk by stumbling and falling. Our progress is curbed by dead ends and disappointments, which no one can entirely escape. Illness and pain, whether of body or mind, are unavoidable. If we are spared serious illness, it touches those who are close to us, and we feel their anguish. From our first love for a pet we are schooled in loss and tragedy, and the lessons do not grow easier with time.

All these facts may seem obvious. Still, within the culture of affluence and "entitlement" it is possible to imagine that suffering is somehow extrinsic to human existence, an unfortunate accident that befalls other people. But such evasion takes us only so far.

Suffering is a fact. The important question is how we face it. As Thomas à Kempis wrote in *The Imitation of Christ*, "The cross always stands ready, and everywhere awaits you. You cannot escape it, wherever you flee; for wherever you go, you bear yourself, and always find youself." He went on to pose these alternatives: "If you bear the cross willingly it will bear you and lead you to your desired goal, where pain shall be no more. . . . If you bear the cross unwillingly, you make it a burden and load yourself more heavily; but you must needs bear it. If you cast away one cross, you will certainly find another, and perhaps a heavier." In a sense those people, including the men and women discussed in this chapter, who come through excruciating experiences not just whole but transformed represent a kind of miracle. We dare not feel at ease at any moment in some sense of reassurance that suffering is really "okay." Those who suffer demand compassion and practical solidarity, not glib solutions to the "problem" of suffering.

Yet we can repeat what the saints learned from experience. By identifying their suffering with the cross of Christ, they found more than consolation; they found a way to transfigure their suffering, binding themselves more intimately to the love of God and to more compassionate union with their neighbors. Here is perhaps the most troubling lesson the saints teach us, yet the most crucial, in our consideration of happiness. We have limited control over the circumstances of our lives. But we have the power in every circumstance to shape our attitudes. Thus, while we can be miserable in the midst of comfort and luxury, it is equally possible—as the saints are witnesses—to be happy in the midst of suffering.

The early church fathers liked to use the image of a mousetrap to describe how God, using Jesus as "bait," contrived to catch Satan. It is a homely image that somewhat dulls the shocking reality of death on a cross. But it resonates with the experience of those saints who, in their suffering, attempted to join themselves to the pattern of Christ. It can speak to us too in our suffering.

The trap has sprung. But we are not caught. The deepest part of our selves is far away, in our true country, beyond the land of thunder, frost, and "falling buildings," at the still center of the turning world.

Seven

LEARNING TO DIE

Do not seek death. Death will find you. But seek the road which makes death a fulfillment.   —Dag Hammarskjöld

God destines all—kings, senators, the powerful of the earth, rich, poor, free men, slaves, great and small, wise and foolish—to death, and after death to judgment. But the ways of dying are not the same.   —St. Apollonius

FROM A CERTAIN point of view it is impossible to reconcile happiness with the thought, much less the reality, of death. A tendency to dwell on death is one of the symptoms of melancholia. Those in its grip are prone to see the cloud in every sky, the shadow of mortality behind every rose. Such persons are generally not the best of company. Against every bit of good news they constantly remind us: "Yes, but tomorrow we shall all be dead." And if this were not actually true, it would not cast such a pall.

At the opposite extreme, of course, there is a manic optimism that denies any sense of mortality. We see it in television commercials, set in the land of eternal youth, or in the faces of people furiously working out in the gym. According to this view, all that matters is that we are alive today. And as long as we avoid secondhand smoke and eat a "heart-healthy diet," we shall keep it that way indefinitely. But this takes us only so far. Authentic life is not "make-believe immortality"; it is always life-in-the-face-of-death. By evading this reality, we may not alter the number of our allotted days, but we pay a price: illusion, dread, an inability to plumb the depths of life or realize its inner meaning.

Death is not simply a future possibility—whether distant or imminent. It is woven into our being from our first breath. As St. Augustine put it, "From the moment a person begins to exist in this body which is destined to die, he is involved all the time in a process whose end is death. . . . Now if each person begins to die, that is to be 'in death,' from the moment when death begins to happen in him then everyone is in death from the moment that he begins his bodily existence."

In this light, we would be wrong to look on death as the end point on an otherwise straight line. Rather, like a question mark that determines the character of a sentence, death is a dimension of everything that precedes it. It transforms our very existence into a question. But we try to evade that question or put it off for a rainy day. As Pascal observed, "Being unable to cure death, wretchedness, and ignorance, men have decided, in order to be happy, not to think about such things." But if that is so, then what we take for happiness is simply a kind of deferred despair.

Leo Tolstoy presented a classic account of this futile evasion in "The Death of Ivan Ilych," the story of a man whose previous life has offered him no adequate preparation for his impending demise. Ivan Ilych, the hero of the story, is a judge who has devoted his life to little else than advancing his career. But just as he achieves the pinnacle of success, a mysterious illness compels him to face his mortality.

Ivan Ilych saw that he was dying, and he was in continual despair. In the depth of his heart he knew that he was dying, but not only was he not accustomed to the thought, he simply did not and could not grasp it. The syllogism he had learnt from Kiesewetter's Logic: "Caius is a man, men are mortal, therefore Caius is mortal," had always seemed to him correct as applied to Caius, but certainly not as applied to himself. That Caius—man in the abstract—was mortal, was perfectly correct. But he was not Caius, not an abstract man, but a creature quite, quite separate from all others. . . . "Caius really was mortal, and it was right for him to die; but for me, little Vanya, Ivan Ilych, with all my thoughts and emotions, it's altogether a different matter. It cannot be that I ought to die. That would be too terrible."

True happiness cannot rest on the determination to avoid unhappy thoughts. That would be like saying that we live in a land of eternal sunshine except when it rains. If our happiness is more than a matter of blissful illusion, it must entail a capacity to face death—not simply the death that will come for Caius, or another abstract mortal, "but for me, little Vanya." To the extent that we can face death without fear or evasion, we can also begin to face life without fear; that is the beginning of happiness, indeed.

Still, there *is* something fearful and terrible about Ivan Ilych's predicament, and more than terrible—truly absurd—if death is simply the End. If the happiness of the saints has rested on a firmer foundation, it is the fact that they did not regard death as the End (except in a relative sense) but as the passage to something new. Dietrich Bonhoeffer, a German theologian executed by the Nazis for his resistance activities, certainly embraced this conviction. After being summoned to the gallows in Flossenberg Prison, he turned to his comrades and said, "This is the end—for us, the beginning of life."

The saints, after all, believed in "the life of the world to come." For many people today this phrase from the Nicene Creed is not an answer but a stumbling block. Though Christians in church pay lip service to the same belief each Sunday, still, the notion of eternal life has as much relation to our normal experience as do castles in the clouds. Perhaps that is because we imagine that eternal life refers to some future reward after all our suffering on earth. As such it is no more than a storybook ending, the equivalent to living "happily ever after." But for the saints who poured out their lives in prayer and service, or who willingly bore the cross of persecution, the motivation was not simply hope of future reward. They believed in eternal life because they had, in some sense, already touched it.

YES TO LIFE

If we are to learn from the saints about how to die—especially those of us whose faith is not so strong—it is a mistake to jump prematurely to the subject of eternal life. It is even a mistake to begin with death. For the saints' attitude toward death was a function of their prior attitude toward life.

On an average day, when the sun is shining, we are prone to regard death as an isolated accident, a dreadful mystery that throws our otherwise stable life into question. But if death is not an accident but an unavoidable aspect of being alive, then it is actually the wider phenomenon of existence that is the real mystery. The question, in other words, is not simply "Why do we die?" but "Why do we live?" Our response determines everything about how we live and how we face the reality of death.

Dag Hammarskjöld, the secretary-general of the United Nations who died in a plane crash in 1961, kept a private journal, a record of his inner life, that was published posthumously under the title *Markings*. It revealed the spiritual journey that quietly underlay his life of public service. In one entry he noted: "I don't know Who—or what—put the question, I do not know when it was put. I don't even remember answering. But at some moment I did answer *Yes* to Someone—or Something—and from that hour I was certain that existence is meaningful and that, therefore, life, in self-surrender, had a goal."

Faith does not usually begin with a set of axioms about "the four last things"—death, judgment, heaven, and hell—to use a once-familiar phrase. Neither does it rest on a set of proofs for the existence of God. It is more likely to begin with an inchoate *Yes* addressed to Someone—or Something—as yet barely known, which implies in turn a certain confidence that life has a meaning and a goal. It becomes our task from that point to discover who that Someone is and what our *Yes* entails.

For the saints that meaning is disclosed, in part, in the life, death, and resurrection of Christ. If the resurrection of Christ reveals the meaning and goal of life, it is because it reveals something essentially true about the nature of reality: that God has erased the boundaries and limits of our existence, that love is stronger than death. . . . And so, by responding to this reality with a fundamental *Yes*, the saints did not merely deposit an attitude to be withdrawn and cashed at the hour of their death; their *Yes* was essentially an attitude directed toward life in the present. It was based on the insight and the experience that new life only begins where our old life ends.

DYING, WE LIVE

Whether it was the apostles Simon and Andrew, who abandoned their fishing nets on the shore, or the would-be disciple who was told to "leave the dead to bury the dead," or the adulteress who was forgiven and told simply to sin no more, there were none who followed Jesus without leaving something behind. This was the basis of Bonhoeffer's comment: "Thus it begins; the cross is not the terrible end to an otherwise God-fearing and happy life, but it meets us at the beginning of our communion with Christ. When Christ calls a man, he bids him come and die."

Bonhoeffer wrote these words in a book published just as the Nazis were establishing the Third Reich. His remarks prefigured his later resistance to Hitler and the price he paid in the waning days of World War II. Under different circumstances he might have formulated his observations more positively, for in every case where the disciples left something behind—whether property, deadness, or sin—it was for the sake of something infinitely more valuable. ("The kingdom of heaven is like treasure hidden in a field, which a man found and covered up; then in his joy he goes and sells all that he has and buys that field" [Matt. 13:44].) It is equally true to say that when Christ calls his followers, he bids them come and *live*.

The intermingling of death and life is a frequent theme in St. Paul's letters. Already in this life, he argues, the disciple has died and been resurrected to new life in Christ: "We know that our old self was crucified with him. . . . But if we have died with Christ, we believe that we shall also live with him" (Rom. 6:5–6). Elsewhere he writes, "For you have died and your life is hid with Christ in God. . . . Put to death therefore what is earthly in you . . . put on then as God's chosen ones, holy and beloved, compassion, kindness, lowliness, meekness, and patience, forbearing one another . . . and above all these put on love" (Col. 3:2).

The image of dying and rising with Christ, not simply at the hour of our death but *today*, this moment, is the key to the sacrament of baptism, the central rite of Christian initiation. Admittedly, the dramatic power of the ritual is attenuated when it is represented by a few sprinkles of water on an infant's brow. Observers might well assume that this ceremony signifies some sort of ritual cleansing. But they would be wrong. It is in fact a symbolic reenactment of the dying and rising of Christ.

This message was undoubtedly more vivid to the early Christians, who gathered in secret in the darkness of the Easter vigil following a season of prayer, fasting, and solemn discernment. By their immersion in the waters of baptism the catechumens (new Christians) marked their death to sin—all the powers of desire and attachment that dragged them down—only to rise to new life, as new selves, constellated by new values. As St. Paul observed, "Do you not know that all of us who have been baptized in Christ Jesus were baptized into his death? We were buried therefore with him by baptism, into death, so that as Christ was raised from the dead by the glory of the Father, we too might walk in newness of life?" (Rom. 5:3–4).

In receiving baptism, the early Christians had a vivid sense that they were dying to "the world," embracing values that made them appear foolish or crazy, if not subversive. They were, after all, proclaiming their affiliation with a crucified Savior, a choice that might well mean sharing in the Savior's fate: arrest, torture, ignominious death. But such a death was only the culmination of a prior, voluntary process of dying to selfishness and sin. In St. Paul's words, "We die each day, and yet behold we live!" (2 Cor. 6:9).

Even as the era of persecution waned, the desert fathers ventured into the wilderness, seeking to lay down their lives in a different arena. Dying to their passions as well as to the values of a world, which, even in the Christian Era, they saw to be marked by avarice, lust, and the thirst for power, they too sought to "walk in newness of life." That impulse was preserved in the later monastic tradition, which continues to the present.

It is reflected in Thomas Merton's description of his first retreat at the Abbey of Gethsemani, the Trappist monastery in Kentucky that later became his home. He wrote how, from the visitors' gallery in the chapel, he noticed a young man dressed in "secular clothes" who stood out conspicuously among the choir monks in their white habits. He was a postulant, someone in the initial stage of becoming a monk. Then one day the young man no longer stood out: "He was in white. They had given him an oblate's habit, and you could not pick him out from the rest. The waters had closed over his head, and he was submerged in the community. He was lost. The world would hear of him no more. He had drowned to our society and become a Cistercian."

Not every conversion is marked by such an abrupt break with the external world. The most immediate change is essentially internal. And yet the element of dying is no less real. St. Augustine, with characteristic irony, depicted his conversion in these terms. While hovering on the edge of faith, he describes himself as held back by the voices of all his sins. "Don't leave us!" they cry out in desperation, already mourning his impending demise. Only on reflection does he realize that this dying to sin is not simply an end but a beginning: "I was dying a death that would bring me life."

Such examples remind us that for the saints, no less than for the rest of us, life and death are related on many levels, long before we face the question of physical death and whatever lies beyond. It is not dying but deadness we should fear. To be sure, there are ways of living that lead to deadness. But at the same time, mysteriously, there is a way of dying that leads to more authentic life. The dying and rising of Christ reveal a kind of code inscribed in the life of faith. When we learn to read that code, we no longer see death as simply the enemy or the End. For with the eyes of faith we see that in all the situations in which we find ourselves there is a path that leads to new and greater life. And in that light it becomes less of a leap to trust that even in the face of physical death God has provided such a path.

Henri Nouwen's sudden death in 1996 at the age of sixty-four caught his friends and family by surprise. He died of a heart attack while passing through Amsterdam on his way to work on a documentary in St. Petersburg. There were numerous ironies at play in this death, the culmination of a "sabbatical" year from his work as chaplain to the Daybreak community in Toronto. Among them was the fact that a man so much afflicted by a sense of homelessness throughout his life should die in his hometown, surrounded in the end by his ninety-year-old father and his siblings. The subject of his planned documentary was his favorite painting: Rembrandt's *Return of the Prodigal Son*.

But perhaps the surprise should not have been so great. Nouwen's posthumously published *Sabbatical Journey* contains abundant evidence of the terrible fatigue that was tugging at his sleeve, even as a restless energy pushed him forward with plans and projects and the quest for deeper answers. It is hard to believe he was not headed for some culminating experience—whether breakthrough or collapse, or both. Yet his friends *were* surprised—even those who traveled to Amsterdam to be at his bedside. As one of them said, "Henri was going to *live*."

In fact Nouwen's writings from the last years of his life make it clear how much he had contemplated and prepared for this particular homecoming. In one journal entry he wrote, "How much longer will I live? . . . Only one thing seems clear to me. Every day should be well lived. What a simple truth! Still, it is worth my attention. Did I offer peace today? Did I bring a smile to someone's face? Did I say words of healing? Did I let go of my anger and resentments?

Did I forgive? Did I love? These are the real questions! I must trust that the little bit of love that I sow now will bear many fruits, here in this world and in the life to come."

These were not random thoughts but the reflections of a man who had devoted unusual attention to the prospect of his own death and had adjusted his entire existential attitude accordingly. The central question was not, How much time remains? but rather, How to prepare for death so that "our dying will be a new way for us to send our and God's spirit to those whom we have loved and who have loved us"?

A particular catalyst for Nouwen's reflections came soon after his move to the Daybreak community when he was nearly killed in a traffic accident. As he walked along a busy highway one wintry day, his mind as usual on other things, he was struck by the side view mirror of a passing van. Although it seemed at first that he had suffered only a few broken ribs, it soon emerged that his internal injuries were life-threatening. But in the hours that followed, as his life hung in the balance, something else happened.

As he later wrote, "I hesitate to speak simply about Jesus, because of my concern that the Name of Jesus might not evoke the full divine presence that I experienced. It was not a warm light, a rainbow, or an open door that I *saw*, but a human yet divine presence that I *felt*, inviting me to come closer and to let go of all fears." As a result, what was on the one hand a terrifying ordeal was also one of the most comforting events of his life. "Death lost its power," he wrote, "and shrank away in the Life and Love that surrounded me in such an intimate way, as if I were walking through a sea whose waves were rolled away. I was being held safe while moving toward the other shore. All jealousies, resentments, and angers were being gently moved away, and I was being shown that Love and Life are greater, deeper, and stronger than any of the forces I had been worrying about."

Anyone familiar with Nouwen's propensity to worry—which is to say, any reader of his previous books—would comprehend the immensity of this statement. And yet the literature of "near-death" experiences is by now so familiar and extensive that Nouwen's account may seem redundant. There is inevitably a gap between one person's life-altering experience of "near death" and the impact of any second-hand account.

Nevertheless, in receiving this "gift of peace," Nouwen felt commissioned to share his new awareness with others. Having touched eternity, he now wondered whether his extra years were not given so that he could "live them from the other side." If theology involves "looking at the world from God's perspective," then perhaps he had been given an opportunity "to live more theologically and to help others to do the same without their having to be hit by the mirror of a passing van."

In previous books Nouwen had taught that our lives belong to others beside ourselves. Now he perceived that this insight applies to our deaths as well. If we die with guilt, shame, anger, and bitterness, all of these become part of our legacy to the world, binding and burdening the lives of our family and friends. It is possible, on the other hand, to regard our dying as a gift, an opportunity to pass along to others our own sense of peace in God.

In many talks on this theme, Nouwen drew on an image taken from his lifelong fascination with the circus. In his later years Nouwen developed a particular friendship with the Flying Rodleighs, a troupe of trapeze artists whom he first encountered in a circus in Holland. For a time he even joined them on the road, filling notebooks with his detailed jottings on every aspect of their craft. He entertained the notion of writing a book about the Flying Rodleighs, believing that in their artistry he might find a new vocabulary for the spiritual life.

He had been particularly fascinated by a remark from one of the flyers, the seeming stars of the trapeze act, who told him that in fact "the flyer does nothing and the catcher does everything." As he explained, "When I fly to [the catcher] I have simply to stretch out my arms and hands and wait for him to catch me and pull me safely over the apron behind the catch bar. . . . A flyer must fly, and a catcher must catch, and the flyer must trust, with outstretched arms, that his catcher will be there for him."

In this circus wisdom Nouwen found a message of great power and consolation. So often we measure our identity and success by how well we remain in control. But in the end the final meaning of our lives may be determined as much by our capacity to trust, to let go, to place ourselves in the hands of Another. In this light, he recalled the words of Jesus on the cross: "Father, into your hands I commend my spirit." "Dying," Nouwen reflected, "is trusting in the catcher."

Some months before his own death, Nouwen was shaken by a particular death in the Daybreak community. It was that of Adam, the severely handicapped young man whom he had cared for during the first year after his arrival at Daybreak, Adam, who had helped him learn, so late in his own life, what it means to be "beloved of God." Finally, after a lifetime of illness and disability, Adam had succumbed to his ailments. It was a testament to the loving care of his community that he had lived to the age of thirty-four. Yet for the L'Arche community, which regards its handicapped members as its "core," Adam's death was a devastating loss. Nouwen rushed back to Toronto from his sabbatical to share the grieving of Adam's family and friends.

Compared with, say, Henri Nouwen, Adam had accomplished nothing, not even the routine tasks that most people take for granted. He could not speak, or dress himself, or brush his teeth. In the eyes of the world the question would not have been why such a man should die but why God had permitted him to live in the first place. Yet Nouwen saw in Adam's life and death a personal reenactment of the gospel story: "Adam was—very simply, quietly, and unquietly—there! He was a person, who by his very life announced the marvelous mystery of our God: I am precious, beloved, whole, and born of God. Adam bore silent witness to this mystery, which has nothing to do with whether or not he could speak, walk, or express himself. . . . It has to do with his being. He was and is a beloved child of God. It is the same news that Jesus came to announce . . . Life is a gift. Each one of us is unique, known by name, and loved by the One who fashioned us."

Jesus too accomplished relatively little during his short public life. He too died as a "failure" in the world's eyes. "Still," Nouwen wrote, "both Jesus and Adam are God's beloved sons—Jesus by nature, Adam by 'adoption'—and they lived their sonship among us as the only thing that they had to offer. That was their assigned mission. That is also my mission and yours. Believing it and living from it is true sanctity."

Nouwen set out to write a book about Adam; it would be his last. He wanted to show, through Adam's life, how each person's story can be understood within the story of Jesus. As was the case with all of Nouwen's best writing, it was also about himself. He seemed to sense in the passing of this young man, as he had in his own brush with death, that he was being called to prepare for his own flight with out-stretched arms—free from gravity, free from all that dis-torted his body and spirit—into the arms of the waiting Catcher. It was as if, he wrote, Adam were saying, "Don't be afraid, Henri. Let my death help you to befriend yours. When you are no longer afraid of your own death, then you can live fully, freely, and joyfully."

It was a voice he had heard before. In another book published, by coincidence, within weeks of his death, he concluded with these words: "Many friends and family members have died during the past eight years and my own death is not so far away. But I have heard the inner voice of love, deeper and stronger than ever. I want to keep trusting in that voice, and be led by it beyond the boundaries of my short life, to where Christ is all in all."

MEMENTO MORI

Time wears different faces. For long periods it stretches out languorously like a cat or passes by with indifferent preci-sion, one thing following another. Yet occasionally there arise those times for which scripture reserves a special word, *kairos*. That is when time rears up to reveal its hidden sig-nificance, a time of crisis that calls for some decisive re-sponse.

Death too wears different faces. There is the abstract and impersonal face that we see in earthquake victims in faraway countries, remote acquaintances, or even celebrities whose obituaries we read in the paper. Perhaps we remark that this is someone we once passed on the street or saw on television. Such a death confronts us with a fleeting reminder of our own mortality, but it remains on the level of an anecdote, something that holds our attention only in passing.

Then there is the face that death presents when it touches us personally, when it draws close to home or steals those to whom we are vitally connected. Then death is no longer simply an anecdote; it has become the crucially important fact that casts a different light on everything we see. Stars, flowers, each innocent creature unaffected by this cataclysm seem to mock us. As King Lear exclaims after the death of Cordelia, "Why should a dog, a horse, a rat, have life, / And thou no breath at all?"

Donald Nicholl, an English Catholic scholar, wrote a moving diary during his final months with terminal cancer. One of the things he remarked was his terrible sense of isolation. For everyone he met, he wrote, his death represented simply one event among many others, "whereas for me my death is *the* event."

Where one stands in relation to this event makes all the difference. The contemplation of death, up close, does not supply new information so much as a new vantage point. The world looks different from there. This change in standpoint can be an occasion of fear, depression, and horror. We may be confronted by how unprepared we are, by the many things we wish we had done differently, by so much we have left unfinished or unresolved. But the approach of death, it is said, can also have a strangely liberating effect. Many people testify that they never felt so fully alive as when facing the prospect of death. So many cares and worries became irrelevant. So many things were clarified or revealed according to their true value. For Father Alfred Delp, a Jesuit hanged by the Nazis in 1945, the anticipation of death brought a new clarity to his deepest convictions. From prison he wrote, "In the course of these last long weeks life has become suddenly much less rigid. A great deal that was once quite simple and ordinary seems to have taken on a new dimension. Things seem clearer and at the same time more profound; one sees all sorts of unexpected angles. And above all God has become almost tangible. Things I have always known and believed now seem so concrete; I believe them but I also live them."

The approach of death may induce panic and fear in even the most stalwart, but it can have other, more positive effects. It can, as Dr. Samuel Johnson noted, "powerfully concentrate the mind," elevating our capacity for spiritual insight and moral discernment. For that reason, a "happy death," according to the saints, is one for which we have had adequate forewarning and preparation. As Flannery O'Connor observed, "Sickness before death is a very appropriate thing and I think those who don't have it miss one of God's mercies."

O'Connor depicted one family's unexpected encounter with death in her short story "A Good Man Is Hard to Find." In this story, a family's innocent outing takes an unfortunate turn when they cross paths with a gang of ruthless criminals. The situation grows worse after the grandmother, a rather silly woman, identifies the ringleader as an escaped convict known as the Misfit. Once recognized, the Misfit has the family led into the woods one at a time to be shot. The grandmother, who is the last to go, carries on a frantic conversation with the Misfit, attempting by turns to appease and distract him. Her thoughtless banter, we are led to conclude, is consistent with her entire life—superficial, naive, oblivious. But at a certain point, as she listens to the Misfit describe his fitful relationship with Jesus, the one who "thown [sic] everything off balance," she experiences a moment of uncharacteristic insight. "Why you're one of my babies," she says, reaching out to touch him on the shoulder. "You're one of my own children!" It is perhaps the most profound gesture of her life. It is also her last, as the Misfit only recoils from her charity with reflexive violence and shoots her dead. "She would have been a good woman," he says, "if she'd of only had someone to shoot her every day of her life."

Ironically, the Misfit's remark echoes the wisdom of earlier spiritual masters, many of whom appreciated the spiritual benefits of an awareness of death. Thomas à Kempis, for example, wrote in *The Imitation of Christ*, "You should order your every deed and thought as though today were the day of your death." Any day, after all, may be our last; thus "always be ready; live in such a way that death can never find you unprepared." At another point he noted, "A man is not only happy but wise also, if he is trying, during his lifetime, to be the sort of man he wants to be found at his death." In a nod to such counsel, many scholars of old liked to keep skulls on their desks as reminders of their mortality. In Europe one can still come across ancient public buildings ornamented, in a similar spirit, with images of scythes, skulls, and scales of judgment. How many people notice them today? At one time these reminders of death, or *memento mori*, served as bells of mindfulness, awakening people to the fleeting nature of their time on earth.

Curiously, such images abounded at a time when there was, arguably, less need for artificial reminders of one's mortality. Given the perils of the premodern age—whether plague, famine, infectious disease, primitive sanitation, or the risks of childbirth—it may be astonishing that any additional signs of death were needed. But from a spiritual point of view, the issue was not simply familiarity with death (which can have its own numbing effect) but rather the virtues and insight that such contemplation might induce.

The anonymous English author of *The Cloud of Unknowing* (another mystical classic of the fourteenth century, written at a time of rampant plague) offered the following advice on how to achieve concentration during prayer: "I think what is going to help you most when you start your prayer—and it doesn't matter whether it is long or short or what—is to make quite sure that you are certain that you will die by the time it is ended, that you will finish before your prayer does!" The author conceded that "almost certainly you will live longer than your prayer, but it is always wrong to bank on it, and a mistake to promise it to yourself."

In other words, whether we acknowledge it or not, we all live with a loaded gun at our heads. If it does not go off today, perhaps it will tomorrow. If not tomorrow, nevertheless it will go off one day. Were today that day, how differently would we behave? If each word and deed bore the weight of our ultimate intention, what would we say? What would we do? Which things would appear most precious and valuable? Which cares would slip from our grasp if we only had someone to shoot us every day of our lives?

Of course, if it took no more than a skull and crossbones to focus our attention, pirates would live in a constant state of enlightenment. We too are surrounded by images and the reality of death, not simply from wars, terrorism, and outbreaks of irrational violence but from the constant soul-numbing possibility of nuclear cataclysm and ecological ruin. Yet in our culture the individual death is largely hidden away, out of view, in hospitals and nursing homes. It figures in our consciousness largely as a statistical possibility—not an impending appointment or a reason to adjust our actions and priorities.

To be sure, if we truly expected death at any moment, there are many otherwise good and necessary things we might fail to accomplish—whether paying our bills or mowing the lawn. Why, for that matter, get out of bed? But meanwhile what of all the good and necessary things—necessary for our happiness, if not our salvation—that we fail to undertake in the unsuspecting confidence that there is "always time"?

Undoubtedly there is a morbid dwelling on death that can dull our capacity for life. But far more common is the fearful preoccupation with avoiding death, a preoccupation that has a similar effect, dulling that dimension of life that calls for wholehearted engagement. A fear of death can easily become a fear of risk, a fear of inconvenience, a fear of the knowledge that might oblige us to act. Thus the specter of death, even when unacknowledged, can make prisoners of us all. One contrasts such fearfulness with the serenity and freedom of St. Thomas More, as he risked death for putting his conscience before loyalty to his king. When his friend the Duke of Norfolk warned him that if he didn't take the Oath of Supremacy (granting King Henry VIII authority over the church in England) he would surely die, More replied: "Well then, I die today, my Lord, and you will die tomorrow."

It is doubtful that the saints, any more than the rest of us, lived in the artificial expectation that each moment might be their last. But through regular reflection on death they sought to be reminded of life's meaning and destination. By living in mindfulness of the value and urgency of each moment, they maintained an acute awareness of themselves and of all that was at stake. The fear of death no longer confined them. They had crossed over to the other side. They had "passed from death to life" (1 John 14). And when death has lost its fearsomeness, all things—even happiness—are possible.

SEEDS OF LIFE

In one of his final reflections, Donald Nicholl wrote, "No one living can teach me about death—no living person has experienced it. . . . The only people who might teach one about death are those who have died, and who in some way have witnessed to the experience. It is the martyrs (witnesses) who at least show us *how* to die. We call upon them and upon the ancestors to take us into their company. What they teach us, above all, is to go into death wholeheartedly, to embrace the experience with one's whole heart and in *joy*."

The original martyrs did indeed embrace their deaths wholeheartedly. The early narratives regularly depict them singing hymns or offering public prayers as they approached their fate, displaying such courage and confidence as to fill even their executioners with wonder and fear, while encouraging the faith of their fellow Christians. This inspired the famous observation of Tertullian, an early Christian theologian, that "the blood of martyrs is the seed of the church."

Certainly, from its earliest days, the church turned to

these martyrs as special guides. Theirs was not just any death, but a death—as was said of the martyrdom of St. Polycarp—"conformable to the gospel," a kind of mystical reenactment of Christ's passion. In laying down their lives for the sake of his name, the martyrs not only imitated Christ's passion but also proclaimed their powerful faith in the resurrection.

But the age of martyrdom did not end with Nero and Diocletian. In almost every corner of the modern world there are examples of men and women who paid the ultimate price for their faith and whose deaths, in that sense, were "comformable to the gospel." And they do have something to teach us. Their stories are remarkable not because they ended, as everyone's must, in death. Nor can we say that they teach us how to overcome all fear of death, for that is not entirely true in every case. But at a bare minimum they do bear witness to one truth, which applies to everyone in whatever circumstances: that the highest purpose of human life is not simply to extend our physical existence for as long as possible. In fact the fear of death tends to recede to the extent that we find and serve "Someone, or Something," as Dag Hammarskjöld might have put it, that we value more dearly than mere longevity.

Martin Luther King, Jr., described this attitude in an interview in 1967. "I live every day with the threat of death," he observed, "and I came to see many years ago that I couldn't function if I allowed fear to overcome me. The main thing is not how long I live, but how well I have acquitted myself in the discharge of these truths that are high, noble, and good."

In fact King reached this conclusion relatively early in his public journey. The critical turning point came late one night in January 1956, when he answered the phone, as his family lay sleeping, and received a particularly vicious death threat. Such calls, as many as forty a day, were commonplace by that time. He had already faced plenty of violence and hatred during the Montgomery bus boycott, the campaign that thrust him into a position of leadership in the black freedom struggle. But somehow the strain of the moment and the implicit threat not only to himself but also to his family brought him to the limit of his strength. He went into the kitchen, and as he sat there with a cup of coffee, he turned himself over to God. As he later recounted, "Almost out of nowhere I heard a voice. 'Martin Luther, stand up for righteousness. Stand up for justice. Stand up for truth. And lo, I will be with you, even until the end of the world.' " Afterward, he said, "I was ready to face anything."

In later years King frequently referred to this episode as his "vision in the kitchen." Such transformative experiences are not uncommon in the lives of the saints. Only when they touch the face of their deepest fears do they find the courage and strength to embark on their mission.

Martin Luther King's subsequent path exposed him to constant danger. Only three days later his house was bombed. He was repeatedly jailed. On one occasion he was nearly fatally stabbed. But he was never again tempted by doubt and despair. Nor did he ever succumb to the temptation to rest on his laurels or to consolidate his popularity at the expense of his prophetic calling. Until the end of his life he continued to reach deeper into the roots of social injustice and hatred and further into the radical challenge of the gospel. All the while he was forging ahead toward his final appointment.

In April 1968 he was in Memphis to lend support to the city's striking sanitation workers. The atmosphere was tense and threatening. Violence was closing in. His famous "dream" seemed increasingly like a nightmare. Nevertheless, on the evening of April 3 he addressed a rally and ended with these words:

> Well, I don't know what will happen now. We've got some difficult days ahead. But it doesn't matter with me now. Because I've been to the mountaintop. And I don't mind. Like anybody, I would like to live a long life. Longevity has its place. But I'm not concerned about that now. I just want to do God's will. And he's allowed me to go up to the mountain. And I've looked over. And I've seen the promised land. I may not get there with you. But I want you to know tonight that we, as a people, will get to the promised land. And I'm happy tonight. I'm not worried about anything. I'm not fearing any man. Mine eyes have seen the glory of the coming of the Lord.

He was assassinated the next day.

To die as a martyr has always been regarded by the church as a special vocation to which few are called and that none should actively seek. But the happiness to which Martin Luther King alluded on the eve of his assassination bears a relevance that is wider than the circumstances of his death. Insofar as it refers to the happiness of the saints, it is largely a matter of inner trust that one is on the right course—no matter how perilous—and that one's soul, and thus one's fate, are in the hands of a loving God. For the saints, it is this confidence, not the assurance of another day or another season, that is the foundation of happiness. As St. Paul said, "None of us lives to himself, and none of us dies to himself.

If we live, we live to the Lord, and if we die, we die to the Lord; so then, whether we live or whether we die, we are the Lord's" (Rom. 14:7–8).

BEFRIENDING DEATH

The word "martyr" comes from the Greek word for "witness." Certainly the martyrs, in laying down their lives, bore witness to Christ and to their confidence in God's promises. In doing so, they also offered an example of how faith may enable a person to face death with courage and serenity. Of course, the martyr's death, usually accompanied by torture and other terror, may seem like an exceptional fate, reserved for a few. But death is seldom unaccompanied by pain and fear. And even under the best of circumstances there is a certain inevitable dread as we contemplate that moment of parting from all that is familiar and friendly to continue on alone. That fact confronts each of us with a similar choice as to the kind of witness we will offer. Thus even those who die from "natural causes" can bear witness and serve as holy martyrs, strengthening and encouraging the faith of others.

Among those who have offered such public witness was Cardinal Joseph Bernardin, the beloved archbishop of Chicago, whose example of courage and serenity in the face of death will doubtless outlive the memory of his many other achievements. At the time of his death in 1996 Bernardin was widely regarded as a leader of the American Catholic church. He had served in a number of prominent roles: as the first general secretary and later the president of the National Conference of Catholic Bishops; as chairman of the commission that drafted the bishops' pastoral letter on nuclear war; as archbishop of Cincinnati, and finally, at age fifty-four, as the cardinal archbishop of Chicago. Among his other contributions, he articulated a "seamless garment" approach to the sacredness of life, a consistent ethic that joined the church's opposition to abortion with rejection of capital punishment and euthanasia, concern for peace and social justice, and a commitment to the poor and most helpless persons in society. That was the public side of his story. But there was another, less visible side.

That story began some years before, when a group of fellow priests confronted him with a challenging question. They asked him to consider whether his life was focused more on the church or on Christ. Their question had a profound impact, causing Bernardin to rethink many of his priorities. He resolved to rise earlier each day to devote more time to prayer. He emptied his savings account and gave everything to the poor. The change was even reflected in his appearance. Once a portly figure, he gradually took on the more gaunt and monastic look of his later years. It was all part of a quiet process of conversion that transformed a successful churchman into a man of God and prepared him for the trials that were to come.

Beginning in 1993, Bernardin was beset by a series of terrible ordeals. It started with a lawsuit by a onetime seminarian from Cincinnati, who claimed he had been sexually abused by Bernardin, his bishop at the time. Though devastated by this accusation, Cardinal Bernardin responded with calm conviction. He utterly denied the charge, while insisting that his case be investigated by the review board he had established for such allegations. He refused to impugn his accuser's character or do anything that might discourage other victims of abuse from coming forward.

The story soon took an astonishing turn, however. The accuser, who had been counseled by an unlicensed therapist, admitted the "unreliability" of his memories and unreservedly withdrew his charges. Though Bernardin's reputation had been indelibly besmirched, he agreed to meet privately with the young man, who was dying of AIDS, celebrated mass with him, and offered his forgiveness.

It was a powerful witness of the gospel, seemingly rewarded with a happy ending. But it was only the beginning of Bernardin's Way of the Cross. Not long after his vindication he called a press conference to announce that he had been diagnosed with pancreatic cancer.

It was typical of Bernardin to want to share this personal information with his "family," the people of Chicago. His candor contrasted with the tradition of public officials, whether in the church or otherwise, to continue issuing reports of excellent health virtually up to the moment of their funerals. He instructed his doctors to hold regular press conferences. Countless American Catholics followed the progress of his surgery, his successive courses of radiation therapy, and other details of his treatment. Along with his regular duties he assumed a new role as an unofficial chaplain to his fellow cancer patients. By the hundreds they reached out to him, asking for his prayers and support. He confided to a friend that in ministering to the sick, he was finding his priesthood again.

Bernardin was determined to impart to others something of his own abiding belief in the sacredness of life and his faith in God's promises. But his gift was all the more valuable for being extended not from an attitude of noblesse oblige but in solidarity with common human frailty. In a pastoral letter to the people of his archdiocese, he wrote that

during his convalescence he "found the nights to be especially long. . . . I sometimes found myself weeping, something I seldom did before. And I came to realize how much
of what consumes our daily life truly is trivial and insignifi-
cant."

In August 1996 he appeared again before the press to
announce that the cancer had spread to his liver and was
deemed inoperable. He had only a few months to live. After
reviewing the procedures for conducting the business of the
archdiocese, he added a personal statement that made a
great impact on the assembled reporters as well as the wider
public: "I can say in all sincerity that I am at peace. I consider this as God's special gift to me at this moment in my
life. We can look at death as an enemy or a friend. If we see
it as an enemy, death causes anxiety and fear. We tend to go
into a state of denial. But if we see it as a friend, our attitude
is truly different. As a person of faith, I see death as a friend,
as a transition from earthly life to life eternal."

The content of this message was unremarkable; it might
have been delivered in any Sunday sermon. But delivered in
such a context and with such authority, it acquired uncommon power. Those who might have recognized in the cardinal's statement the influence of Henri Nouwen would not
have been mistaken. Bernardin later described how much he
had been helped by a visit from Nouwen, who spoke to him
about death as a friend and left him a copy of his book *Our
Greatest Gift*. (It is a reminder of life's contingency that
Nouwen, who came to offer comfort to the dying archbishop, would unexpectedly precede him in death that very
year.) Bernardin certainly embraced the message of that
book and showed in an extraordinary fashion what it means
to make of one's death a gift for others.

Among the efforts of his final months was the decision to write his own book, *The Gift of Peace*, "to help others understand how the good and the bad are always present in our human condition and, that if we 'let go,' if we place ourselves totally in the hands of the Lord, the good will prevail." That task of trusting and letting go, he said, was a lifelong process, one that continued until life's end.

In a speech in September 1996 he said, "As a bishop I have tried . . . to shape a moral message about the unique value of human life and our common responsibilities for it. As my life slowly ebbs away, as my temporal destiny becomes clearer each hour and each day, I am not anxious, but rather reconfirmed in my conviction about the wonder of human life, a gift that flows from the very being of God and is entrusted to each of us."

In his last weeks, with his candle burning visibly shorter, Bernardin received a great outpouring of affection and admiration, and not simply from his fellow Catholics. *Newsweek* carried his picture on the cover with the headline "Teaching Us How to Die." People of every faith, and even confirmed agnostics, were moved by the spectacle of a frail but faithful man offering the greatest gift and witness simply by the manner of his death.

Cardinal Bernardin died on November 14, 1996. On the day of his funeral the city of Chicago came to a halt. But his teaching continued. When his book was published, it quickly became a national bestseller. In words he had written just days before his passing he noted that spring would follow winter. "It is quite clear that I will not be alive in the spring," he wrote. "But I will soon experience new life in a different way. Although I do not know what to expect in the afterlife, I do know that just as God has called me to serve him to the best of my ability through my life on earth, he is now calling me home."

BEFORE AND AFTER

St. Bede, an eighth-century English monk (the Venerable Bede, as he is called), wrote a famous history of the English church. In one chapter he described a critical point in the conversion of King Edwin of Northumbria in the seventh century. After listening to the appeal of St. Paulinus, a wandering missionary, and still wavering on the question of whether he should accept the new Christian faith, King Edwin called in his council of wise men to seek their advice. One of them spoke thus:

> Your Majesty, when we compare the present life of man with that time of which we have no knowledge, it seems to me like the swift flight of a lone sparrow through the banqueting hall where you sit in the winter months to dine with your thanes and counselors. Inside there is a comforting fire to warm the room; outside, the wintry storms of snow and rain are raging. This sparrow flies swiftly in through one door of the hall, and out through another. While he is inside, he is safe from the winter storms; but after a few moments of comfort, he vanishes from sight into the darkness whence he came. Similarly, man appears on earth for a little while, but we know nothing of what went before this life, and what follows. Therefore if this new teaching can reveal any more certain knowledge, it seems only right that we should follow it.

King Edwin was subsequently baptized, along with all his thanes, counselors, and other subjects.

Christianity is not alone in proposing answers to, if not more certain knowledge about, the mystery of our existence. Many philosophers and religious teachers have addressed these questions about the source, meaning, and destiny of human existence. What was new about the preaching of St. Paulinus and other missionary saints was their claim that in the death and resurrection of one man—albeit the Son of God—the veil was lifted from our future destiny. For those who put away sin—the weight of deadness—and put on the spirit of Christ, death was no longer a fearful enemy. And this faith allowed such men and women to live in a new spirit, embracing life, yet trusting that the short span of their existence was but a kind of small harbor open to the mysterious depths beyond.

More than a thousand years later the questions pondered by King Edwin and his retinue continue to trouble restless seekers. For many, the Christian answers, worn smooth by too much casual handling, have lost their power to surprise and enlighten. For a generation accustomed to the pace of music videos the notion of eternal life—or eternal anything, for that matter—may sound like a colossal bore.

But there are others, perhaps having explored various philosophies and religious paths, who are prepared to listen anew to the saints, those best qualified by experience and conviction to represent the wisdom of Christianity, to see if they can reveal any more certain knowledge. They will find that the saints were not only teachers but also fellow seekers.

In a crowded lecture hall at Yale, Henri Nouwen once wrote on the blackboard the date of his birth, 1932, followed by a short line to another date, 2010, which was followed by a question mark. "This could represent my life," he told the audience, "a finite period with a beginning and an end." (Neither he nor his listeners could guess how much shorter the actual line would be.) Then he shook his head. Returning to the blackboard he drew a line, straight as the flight of a sparrow, from one end of the blackboard all the way across to the other. Then he said, "I have come from somewhere and I am going someplace else."

As Nouwen realized, the question of King Edwin's wise man is not really answered by disclosing the destination of that sparrow in the banquet hall but by comprehending the continuity of its flight. The source of our existence is God— so the Christian tradition teaches—and God is our ultimate destination. Our task in life—whether it is short or long, whether it is heavy with sorrows or light with blessings, or, like most lives, a combination of the two—is to find the path that conveys us toward our true destination.

Neither fame nor riches nor great achievements will cross with us to the other side. Resentments, bitterness, anger, and regrets will not serve us, though many cling to them as if to gold; to carry them with us would be hell indeed. Either we must learn to let go or be stripped of all that weakens our capacity to love with single hearts. It is less painful to let go. Death will finish the job that we have left incomplete.

Eight

LEARNING TO SEE

The eyes of the world see no farther than this life, as mine
see no farther than this wall when the church door is shut.
The eyes of the Christian see deep into eternity.
— St. John Vianney, the Curé d'Ars

ONE MIGHT HAVE ASSUMED that with "Learning to
Die" we had reached the last chapter in any guide to happiness. That, after all, is where our earthly journey ends. "The
rest," as Hamlet said, "is silence." But the saints have more
to teach us. In their eyes neither life nor our vocation to happiness ends with death. We are created for a happiness
greater than this life can contain. And so the aim of the spiritual life is to orient us toward that goal and in that light to
weigh our desires, our actions, and our sufferings, according
to their true value.

Traditionally the church has described that goal, the
achievement of our final happiness, as an act of *seeing*, the
Beatific Vision, the direct encounter with God. That vision is
characterized first of all by its unmediated clarity. As St. Paul
wrote, "We see now as though in a mirror dimly, but then

face to face" (1 Cor. 13:12). It is also a kind of seeing that changes us, realigning our very hearts and wills to the object of our sight.

Dante described this vision in the conclusion of the *Divine Comedy*:

> O grace abounding and allowing me to dare
> to fix my gaze on the Eternal Light,
> so deep my vision was consumed in It!
>
> I saw how it contains within its depths
> all things bound in a single book by love
> of which creation is the scattered leaves. . . .
>
> I know I saw the universal form,
> the fusion of all things, for I can feel
> while speaking now, my heart leap up in joy. . . .

Dante's work describes an imaginative pilgrimage from the depths of hell, up the mount of purgatory, and finally to the ethereal rapture of paradise. When the poet reaches his destination, he is led to gaze on the Trinity itself, a dazzling light, like three rainbows reflecting one upon another. As he strives to penetrate this mystery, his mind suddenly receives a "great flash of understanding" until, as he writes, "like a wheel in perfect balance turning, / I felt my will and my desire impelled / by the Love that moves the sun and the other stars."

With such language Christian artists have attempted to depict a state of happiness that necessarily defies description. Since Dante's time that image has been updated in numerous paintings, poems, and films, from Botticelli to *Paradise Lost* to *A Guy Named Joe*. Meanwhile the unfolding of modern physics, along with explorations of outer space, has enriched our understanding of the forces that "move the sun and the other stars." Still, questions remain that neither science nor art can answer. Is there such a thing as perfect happiness? If so, how does such *ultimate* happiness relate to life "as we know it"? Is there a way of seeing *now* that connects us, in whatever degree, to that blessed vision of Dante's imagination?

One answer comes from the mystics and visionaries, with their descriptions of fantastic journeys beyond the doors of perception. But most of the saints enjoyed no visions at all, except perhaps, as Dorothy Day admitted, "visions of unpaid bills and dirty dishes." Yet with the eyes of faith they discerned an extra dimension even in the most prosaic circumstances. St. Augustine believed that all things true and lovely and good serve as a lure, drawing us toward their ultimate source. It is *this* orientation—toward the Source, even though only dimly perceived—that characterizes the saints. It is this orientation that allows us too to see beneath the drab surface of history, commerce, and nature, to what Gerard Manley Hopkins called "the dearest freshness deep down things."

To see these things is not a matter of looking in special "religious" places; we need only learn to see in a different way, with different eyes. "Our whole business in this life," according to St. Augustine, "is to restore to health the eyes of the heart, whereby God may be seen." Such vision is otherwise known as faith. All the saints had it, and it is the presupposition in every lesson in their guide to happiness. For in seeing with the eyes of faith, they were confident of living in a wider reality that gave purpose to their actions and attitudes: their work, their love, their silence, their sorrows. That was the source of their happiness, as it is the source of our happiness too, if we undertake to learn from their example.

ALL THE WAY TO HEAVEN

Many theologians, preachers, and artists have imagined the happiness of the saints in heaven. Relatively little attention, by contrast, has focused on the happiness of the saints on earth. In fact some have questioned whether true happiness in this life is an attainable or even a desirable goal.

Many Catholics, though ever fewer, can still recite from memory the opening lines of the Baltimore Catechism:

Who made you? God made me.
Why did God make you? To know, love, and serve Him in this world so as to be happy with Him forever in the next.

If the traditional catechism ignored the possibility of being happy *in this world*, that was no casual oversight. It reflected a long-standing tendency to regard the present life as merely instrumental, a means to attain a greater goal. That goal, "eternal happiness," was by definition beyond the reach of mortal beings.

In the *Summa Theologica* St. Thomas Aquinas devoted considerable attention to this question, largely to show why happiness, in its ultimate sense, can refer to "nothing else than the vision of the Divine essence." After reviewing in turn such ephemeral goods as wealth, honor, fame, power, health, and pleasure, he showed how vain it was to suppose that any of these could provide perfect happiness. Indeed, in setting forth his proofs, Aquinas kept his eye so resolutely trained on "perfect" happiness as to imply that anything short of that goal was hardly worth the name.

But in thus focusing on our future goal, Aquinas was heir to a long tradition. Our life on earth, according to this perspective, is conceived as a state of "lonely exile" from our true country. In the words of the "Salve Regina," a medieval hymn in honor of the Virgin, we are "poor, banished children of Eve, weeping and mourning in this vale of tears." The effort to be happy in this life is not only vain but positively harmful to the extent that it causes us to forget who we are and where we are headed.

According to St. Augustine, everything serves a good and valuable purpose to the extent that it helps us attain our final destination. But too much happiness in this life poses the risk that we will become fixated on the "means" and lose sight of our true goal. "Suppose we were wanderers who could not live in blessedness except at home, miserable in our wandering and desiring to end it and to return to our native country. We would need vehicles for land and sea that could be used to help us to reach our homeland. . . . But if the amenities of the journey and the motion of the vehicle itself delighted us, and we were led to enjoy those things that we should use, we should not wish to end our journey quickly, and, entangled in a perverse sweetness, we should be alienated from our country, whose sweetness would make us blessed."

Doubtless there is merit to Augustine's caution. It is true that in this life we have no abiding home, and we should therefore live with a view to what is ultimately important.

And for those who need persuading that "perfect happiness" is unattainable on earth, Augustine and Aquinas bear a cogent warning. But is this the only important warning? Is it the one we most need to hear?

In the midst of pain and hardship it may be encouraging to place our hopes in a future life in which every sorrow will be comforted, every tear wiped dry. But there is good reason to be suspicious of spiritual prescriptions that dismiss all the blessings of this life, "the amenities of the journey," in favor of some ideal paradise to come. At best such attitudes may foster indifference and passivity; at worst, a cold fanaticism. At the very least, they smack of ingratitude.

Even writing from a prison cell, Dietrich Bonhoeffer resisted this temptation. "I believe we ought so to love and trust God in our lives and in all the good things that he sends us, that when the time comes (but not before) we may go to him with love, trust, and joy. But, to put it plainly, for a man in his wife's arms to be hankering after the other world is, in mild terms, a piece of bad taste, and not God's will."

Though heaven may represent the perfection of our happiness, it is not by way of death but by way of holiness that we get there. So the saints have taught. What does this mean? That we prepare for heaven by a life of steady acclimation to the love and goodness of God; that the way to heaven begins where we are standing. . . . And if this is so, we must acknowledge that life on Earth is not simply a vale of tears. There is also a true sweetness to *this life* that, if we could only see and acknowledge it, might make us happy *and* blessed.

Some saints have emphasized the deep chasm separating the perfect happiness of heaven from its shadowy counter-

parts in our everyday lives. But many others have acknowledged the lines of continuity. As even Aquinas conceded,
"Men esteem that there is some kind of happiness to be had
in this life, on account of a certain likeness to true Happiness. And thus they do not fail altogether in their estimate."

For Aquinas the connecting link was contemplation, by
which we draw ever closer to the essence of God. On the
other hand, for St. Brigid of Ireland, a sixth-century abbess
who embodied a somewhat earthier brand of holiness, the
link lay in the practice of hospitality. She envisioned heaven
as a large family gathered around a lake of beer. Two different saints, two different paths. Regardless of the differences,
in the lives of many saints there have been moments of insight when that seeming chasm between "here" and "hereafter" evaporated, when it became clear, as St. Catherine of
Siena wrote, that "all the way to Heaven is Heaven."

SHINING LIKE THE SUN

Thomas Merton achieved early fame through the publication of *The Seven Storey Mountain*. But in some ways that
fame became a burden. In the public mind he was eternally
fixed at the point where his memoir ended: a young monk
with his cowl pulled over his head, happily convinced that
in joining an austere monastic community, he had fled the
world, never to return. It was difficult for readers to appreciate that this picture represented only the beginning of Merton's journey as a monk. In later years he wrote, with much
exasperation, "*The Seven Storey Mountain* is the work of a
man I never even heard of."

One aspect of the book that he particularly came to regret was the attitude of pious scorn directed at the "world" and its unfortunate citizens. He had seemed to regard the monastery as a haven set apart from this *massa damnata*. Only with time had he realized that "the monastery is not an 'escape' from the world. On the contrary, by being in the monastery I take my true part in all the struggles and sufferings of the world." With this realization his writing assumed an increasingly compassionate and ecumenical tone.

In one of his published journals he described a moment of mystical awareness that marked a critical turning point in his life as a monk. It occurred during an errand into nearby Louisville, "at the corner of Fourth and Walnut in the center of the shopping district. I was suddenly overwhelmed with the realization that I loved all those people, that they were mine and I theirs, that we could not be alien to one another even though we were total strangers. It was like waking from a dream of separateness, of spurious self-isolation in a special world, the world of renunciation and supposed holiness."

Merton had discovered a sense of solidarity with the human race—not simply in shared sin but also in grace—and he described this as an awakening to genuine happiness. "There is no way of telling people that they are all walking around shining like the sun," he wrote. "There are no strangers! . . . The gate of heaven is everywhere."

No doubt many influences converged in this insight, enabling Merton to break through the limits of a certain narrow religious perspective. Yet it seems clear that this experience in Louisville was a crucial event, a moment in which everyday reality appeared "transfigured" in a way that permanently affected his vision.

In the same passage he discussed what he called "the

point vierge," a point of pure truth at the center of our being, "which belongs entirely to God." Using language traditionally reserved for the Beatific Vision, he described this point, in which God's glory is inscribed in our being: "It is like a pure diamond, blazing with the invisible light of heaven. It is in everybody, and if we could see it we would see these billions of points of light coming together in the face and blaze of a sun that would make all the darkness and cruelty of life vanish completely."

TRANSFIGURATION

Merton's epiphany at Fourth and Walnut has parallels in the lives of many saints and mystics. One recalls Julian of Norwich's vision of the world as a precious hazelnut in the hand of God, or the event described by St. Hildegard of Bingen, a twelfth-century German mystic, when "a fiery light flashed from the open vault of heaven. It permeated my brain and enflamed my heart and the entire breast not like a burning, but like a warming flame, as the sun warms everything its rays touch." Through such occurrences the mystics commonly speak of awakening to the meaning of scripture, or the destiny of the universe, or simply the resplendent heart of the everyday world. What they share is some flash of insight in which the outer curtain of reality is drawn aside to reveal, if only for a moment, a vision of what is truly inside.

In each of these experiences there is an echo of that mysterious incident described in the gospels and afterward commemorated as the Transfiguration of Christ. On that occasion Jesus led three of his disciples—Peter, James, and John—up a mountain, where he was suddenly "transfigured before them, and his garments became glistening, intensely white, as no fuller on earth could bleach them." It is one of the most remarkable stories in scripture, one of the few times when the disciples were not forced to contend with figures and parables but were afforded a glimpse of the *thing* itself—whatever that is: Christ in his future glory? Some kind of insight into the deeper heart of reality? Only Peter could speak through his fear and astonishment: "Lord, it is good to be here." But suddenly the moment passed, and it was time to return home. And all the way down the mountain the disciples mumbled to one another about what they had seen and what it meant.

In the typical life such epiphanies come infrequently, if at all, and that is probably for the best. Most of us are no more equipped to face the naked truth than we are to stare at the sun. As Georges Bernanos wrote, "I don't suppose if God had given us the clear knowledge of how closely we are bound to one another, both in good and evil, that we could go on living." Nevertheless, we recall certain moments in our lives when everything appeared completely clear and vivid. It may have been a chance encounter that proved decisive in the unfolding of our lives or an intimate conversation that cut to the heart of things. Suddenly the veil of everydayness was pulled aside, and we sensed that we were standing on holy ground.

What did we do with these experiences? In most cases we probably walked away or brushed them from our minds, lest they interfere with our routine plans and the business we call reality. But for the saints such experiences were the true touchstone of reality, the constellation by which they charted their course.

The decisive moment could be something simple. For

Brother Lawrence of the Resurrection the turning point came after his long service in the French army. As a veteran of the Hundred Years War he had witnessed who knows what horrors. Then, one cold midwinter day, he happened to look upon a gaunt and leafless tree. He could see that in a little time the bare branches of this tree would again be covered with leaves, and this thought suddenly filled him with "a high view of the providence and power of God." There was a direct path from this insight to his later entry into a Carmelite monastery in Paris, where he cultivated his "practice of the presence of God."

For others the key moment might occur through an ethical challenge or a particular encounter with human suffering. One of the earliest biographies of a saint is the life of St. Martin of Tours, a fourth-century bishop who at one time served as a tribune in the Roman army in France. One day he encountered a poor beggar, dressed in rags and shivering in the cold. Martin, who was seated on his horse and dressed in the regalia of his office, responded by removing his own cloak. With his sword he cut the garment in two, gave one half to the beggar, and wrapped himself in the other. That night, the story goes, he dreamed he saw Jesus wearing the part of the cloak he had given away. The following day, at the risk of his life, he resigned his commission and sought baptism as a Christian. "I am a soldier of Christ," he told his superiors. "It is not lawful for me to fight."

The moment of awakening could occur through an encounter with another saint. In the case of St. Edith Stein, a Jewish-born German philosopher who became a Carmelite nun and who eventually perished in Auschwitz, the crucial moment came after she had stayed up all one night reading the autobiography of St. Teresa of Ávila. As the sun rose on a new morning, she put down the book and exclaimed, "This is the truth!"

Such moments of discovery may be brief, but their effects endure. Though memory may dim, the knowledge that once, even if only for a moment, we have touched the truth, means that we are living in a wider world.

TRANSCENDENCE

Augustine describes such a moment in his *Confessions*. It occurred in the course of a conversation with his mother, Monica, just after his conversion and only days before her death. For years Monica had suffered over her errant son, praying constantly for his conversion. She had lived for one purpose: to see him baptized. Now, with this goal fulfilled, mother and son found themselves conversing one afternoon on the happiness of the saints: "We were wondering what the eternal life of the saints would be like, that life which no eye has seen, no ear has heard, no human heart conceived. But we laid the lips of our hearts to the heavenly stream that flows from Your fountain, the source of all life which is in You, so that as far as it was in our power to do so we might be sprinkled with its waters and in some sense reach an understanding of this great mystery."

As their conversation progressed, they came to the conclusion that no bodily pleasure or earthly delight was worthy of comparison or even mention "beside the happiness of the life of the saints." And as "the flame of love burned stronger" between them, raising them higher, toward the eternal God, their thoughts "ranged over the whole compass of material things in their various degree, up to the heavens themselves, from which the sun and the moon and the stars shine down upon the earth."

Oblivious of the passage of time, they continued their ascent. "Higher still we climbed, thinking and speaking all the while in wonder at all that you have made. At length we came to our own souls and passed beyond them to that place of everlasting plenty, where you feed Israel for ever with the food of truth."

Still their conversation went on, rising ever higher: "And while we spoke of the eternal Wisdom, longing for it and straining for it with all the strength of our hearts, for one fleeting instant we reached out and touched it."

It was one of those brief mountaintop experiences, the kind that melts away as soon as we reach out to grasp it. As Augustine relates, "Then with a sigh, leaving our spiritual harvest bound to it, we returned to the sound of our own speech, in which each word has a beginning and an ending— far, far different from your word, our Lord, who abides in himself for ever, yet never grows old and gives new life to all things."

Not many even aspire to touch that infinite realm of light and beauty. But in the lives of many ordinary people it is still possible to recall times when they found themselves in the presence of something awesome and transcendent, something that moved them to utter, if only to themselves, "This is the truth!"

In recounting the story of her conversion, Dorothy Day included such an incident from her childhood in Chicago. She recalled how one morning she went to visit a little girl named Kathryn Barrett, who lived next door. Seeing no one on the porch or in the kitchen, where breakfast dishes lay neatly washed, Dorothy burst into one of the bedrooms. There she found Kathryn's mother on her knees, praying. Seemingly undisturbed by the interruption, Mrs. Barrett turned to Dorothy and told her that Kathryn and the other children had gone to the store. Then she went on with her praying.

As Day wrote, "I felt a burst of love toward Mrs. Barrett that I have never forgotten." Even after many years the memory of this casual encounter remained. And though Day later become absorbed in the problems of poverty and injustice, still, "there were moments when, in the midst of misery and class strife, life was shot through with glory. Mrs. Barrett in her sordid little tenement flat finished her breakfast dishes at ten o'clock in the morning and got down on her knees and prayed to God."

This small incident was among the many influences that contributed to Day's eventual conversion. In describing the process, she assigned a special role to the birth of her daughter, Tamar. But it was not just the experience of happiness that turned her heart to God. It was also the apprehension of something lacking in her own life, something she had observed among her neighbors, the poor immigrants whose cause, as a radical, she had eagerly championed. Most of these people were faithful Catholics. As such, she perceived, they lived in the presence of truths and values that gave their lives meaning beyond the sum of their material circumstances.

In the years that followed her conversion—even after, with the help of Peter Maurin, she had found her calling and her home in the Catholic Worker movement—Day still encountered loneliness and sorrow. She continued to "groan over the hideous sordidness of man's fate." But she never lost touch with a deep instinct for the holiness in all things. She believed, by virtue of the Incarnation, that every corner of life, whether beautiful or squalid, was touched by grace. Everything human and everything in nature—the howl of an animal in the night, the breezes on the bay, the creeping vine on a tenement fire escape—spoke to her of God. And she never ceased to believe, despite the hardships and insecurity she endured, that life in community affords a glimpse and foretaste of the heavenly banquet. When asked about her work and what she was trying to achieve, she answered simply: "We are trying to make people happy."

BEATIFIC VISION

St. Augustine concluded his book *The City of God* with an extended reflection on the activity of the saints in heaven. He was particularly intrigued by St. Paul's promise that there we shall see God "face to face." What this meant Augustine could only speculate. Will the saints see God with their bodily eyes, "in the same way as we now see the sun, moon, stars, sea, and death and all things on the earth"? This, he conceded, "is no easy question." Perhaps, he suggested, we shall see through the "eyes of the heart," so that even if our eyes are shut, wherever we turn our spiritual eyes, we may see God "directing the whole universe."

Still, we return to our earlier questions: Is this *true*? Is such happiness possible? What does it have to do with our present life, our desire to find happiness now?

For each person the idea of heaven may inspire a different image, whether shaped by Dante's poetry or by greeting-card pictures of cherubs sitting on a cloud. Tastes vary, and so do conceptions of the state in which our desire for ultimate happiness achieves its fulfillment. There is no reason to suppose that a farmer's, a cabdriver's, a rodeo performer's image of heaven must reflect the conceptions of Dante and Thomas Aquinas. Yet regardless of our images, we can be sure of one thing: that we cannot locate such a place on any map of the cosmos; we cannot demonstrate its reality with any rational proof.

And so *is it true?* It is impossible to answer that question from the outside, from the perspective of detached and neutral science or argumentation. The truths of the gospel do not appeal to objective proof but to personal commitment; they are verified not by logical syllogisms, but only by living experience. Thus to the disciples' objective question "Where are you staying?" Jesus replied with an invitation to discipleship: "Come and see" (John 1:39).

Fortunately, there are ways of knowing apart from reason. That is where faith enters in—what St. Paul described as "the substance of things hoped for, the evidence of things unseen." Though we cannot adopt their experience secondhand, still we can mark the testimony of the saints. They report that with the eyes of faith they perceived God, but they also perceived the world and this ordinary life in a different light. As Jean-Pierre de Caussade observed, "Faith transforms the earth into paradise. By it our hearts are raised with the joy of our nearness to heaven."

"Wherever God is, there is Heaven," wrote St. Teresa of Ávila. And since God is everywhere, we can see how daily life itself can truly become the road to heaven, the path to our happiness. In learning to see with the eyes of faith, we are preparing ourselves by degrees for that final happiness, described by St. Augustine in the closing hymn of *The City of God*: "There we shall be still and see; we shall see and we shall love; we shall love and we shall praise."

The life of faith is not necessarily a life spent in a monastery or in church. Nevertheless, most of the saints did engage in a course of disciplined religious practice. They prayed at set hours, rose early to reflect on scripture, performed the rosary, engaged in regular examinations of conscience, submitted to the counsel of spiritual directors or religious superiors. They joined with others in a community of faithful practice; they followed the liturgical calendar of fasting, renewal, and celebration; they studied the lives of the saints, went on pilgrimage, received the sacraments. All these were tools, habits to awaken and train the eyes of faith. But their point in undertaking such exercises was not to block out everything in life that distracted them from God. It was to achieve the condition in which nothing distracted them from God.

The old catechism spoke of "knowing, loving, and serving God in this world so as to be happy with Him forever in the next." What was puzzling and unsatisfying about this statement was its apparently arbitrary causality. It suggested that heaven, or happiness, was a "reward" for our holiness in this life. But is there no other connection apart from cause and effect? The catechism makes much more sense if the way of holiness is also the way of happiness, if eternity simply seals the option we have made and pursued in this life.

In one of his sermons John Henry Newman, the great Victorian theologian, asked why it is necessary to be holy to enter heaven. Might not God just as easily have established another standard, perhaps one with wider concession to our weaknesses?

Newman answered, "Even supposing a man of unholy

life were suffered to enter heaven, *he would not be happy there*; so that it would be no mercy to permit him to enter." For heaven is a matter of being in the presence of God, of finding pleasure in God's will. Where there is no such pleasure, there can be no happiness. Holiness therefore is not some arbitrary winning ticket that earns us passage into heaven. "Heaven is *not* heaven," Newman put it, "is not a place of happiness *except* to the holy."

Heaven is *not* heaven *except* to the holy. But in walking the path of holiness, the saints perceived, with Thomas Merton, that "the gate of heaven is everywhere." In that light we can say that this life too becomes "a place of happiness" to the extent that we grow in holiness and learn to see with the eyes of faith. This was the insight of Dostoevsky's holy Father Zossima: "Gentlemen, look around you at the gifts of God, the clear sky, the pure air, the tender grass, the birds; nature is beautiful and sinless, and we, only we, are sinful and foolish, and we don't understand that life is heaven, for we have only to understand that and it will at once be fulfilled in all its beauty, we shall embrace each other and weep."

The saints have spoken of the *memento mori*, the reminder of death, and how this heightens our sense of spiritual urgency. But there is also a *memento dei*, an awareness of God, that can be cultivated at all times and in all circumstances.

In this spirit, a Dutch Carmelite priest named Titus Brandsma, arrested and later killed by the Nazis for defending the Jews, smuggled this message out of Dachau: "I see God in the work of his hand and the marks of his love in every visible thing and it sometimes happens that I am seized by a supreme joy which is above all other joys."

This awareness, above all, is so necessary in our world. It promotes the conviction that life, despite all the forces of irrationality and cruelty, is ultimately meaningful and good. It fosters the confidence that happiness is truly possible. It supports the hope, as Julian of Norwich put it, that "all shall be well, and all shall be well, and all manner of things shall be well."

CONCLUSION

Travelers on the road to God's wisdom find that the further they go, the more the road opens out, until it stretches to infinity.   —Origen

I HAVE SPENT much of my life reading books about saints: medieval legends, spiritual memoirs, martyrologies, and manuals of devotion. If that is all it takes to be happy then, as Thomas Merton says, "I should have been a very happy person, a spiritual millionaire, from the cradle even until now." Yet with happiness, as with holiness, it is not what we read but what we practice that makes the difference.

Each day brings new failures. I become impatient; I worry about small things and take other people for granted; I give in to distractions and remain inattentive to signs of grace; I daydream about heroic deeds, while neglecting countless opportunities for charity.

And yet, like everyone else, I yearn to be happy. This desire is one of the marks of being human, a sign that we are called to a more abundant life. No less than others, I have looked for happiness in one place or another, imagining it would follow once I had realized some ambition or had resolved a looming crisis. But experience has only confirmed the wisdom of the saints, both those I have studied and those I have known, whose happiness did not hinge on passing feelings or outward circumstances. They have shown that the true happiness we all desire is the other side of the holiness to which we are called. The two proceed from the same practice and converge on the same goal.

If holiness were the same as genius or moral perfection, then this goal would concern only a very few. But holiness is not about possessing "the right stuff." Nor is it a code or prescription we must follow. It is more like a habit of being, a certain fullness of life, or "loveliness of the spirit." It is a name for that quality by virtue of which all things or persons fulfill their purpose and reason for being. Yet it does not just "happen." Such holiness, as the preceding chapters describe, is the fruit of considerable work and practice.

On this path we are never *finished*. We remain always and only on the way. For that reason, instead of talking about "saints" as if they represented some kind of different creature, we might prefer to speak of "those who walk the paths of holiness." At once we have a sense of what unites us with the saints, our fellow travelers, much deeper than all that sets us apart. We are all saints "in progress," to the extent that we desire to be. Some, to be sure, progress farther than others. But St. Paul made no distinctions when he addressed his readers as saints. They were saints by virtue of their calling to be saints.

By the same token there is no way *to* happiness. But there is a way *of* happiness, a way of lightness and balance, a way that allows us to take in experience and give it back with humanity and forgiveness, a way that awakens us to the particularity of each moment as well as its sacred depths. So often we proceed as though looking through a "mental telescope," trained above the heads of our fellow humans, and what we see seems petty, commonplace, and meaningless. But then comes a moment when our yearning for happiness joins paths with the call to holiness. In the focus that ensues, we see the world in a new light. And in that light ordinary life becomes not only infinitely valuable but radiant and engrossing.

✦

The significance of these ideas was affirmed for me as I neared completion of this book, when I received word that an old friend was dying of cancer.

I had met Chuck Matthei twenty-eight years before, when he appeared one night at my college dorm room. I hadn't known who he was or where he came from, but his visit was well timed. Since turning eighteen that winter, I had been undergoing a private crisis about whether to register for the draft. In those waning days of the Vietnam War scarcely anyone I knew could comprehend why this was something to worry about. But Chuck understood. Having somehow heard about my dilemma, he had hitchhiked across the state to meet me.

As I later learned, this was characteristic behavior. Chuck was drawn like a magnet to any young person at a moral crossroad. Whatever the issue, he came to share his own experience and to support whatever instinct had led someone to probe more deeply into the meaning and purpose of life.

To say that Chuck made a strong impression would be an

understatement. His full Viking beard and prematurely balding head, as much as the authority in his voice, made him seem much older than his years. (He was twenty-five.) One could hardly fail to be swept up in his energy, his sense of mission, and his vision of a better world. I had never met anyone like him.

We talked all that night, as he described his philosophy and his journey. I heard about how he had faced his own crossroad, deciding to forgo college, burning his draft card, and taking up the life of an itinerant peacemaker. As consistently as he could, he lived by the spirit of nonviolence, inspired by such figures as Gandhi, Tolstoy, Thoreau, and Dorothy Day. His great theme was the freedom we always possess to shape our response and attitude, despite the circumstances in which we find ourselves.

I learned that he was the strictest sort of vegetarian—a vegan—who fasted one day a week and did most of his grocery shopping out of supermarket Dumpsters. He had no possessions to speak of. This asceticism had a moral component. But it was also a matter of training and discipline, a readiness for whatever sacrifice might be necessary. (That discipline was particularly tested on those occasions when he was arrested and refused to walk or eat in jail.) But there was nothing dour or moralistic about him. As St. Athanasius said of St. Antony, "He was never troubled, his soul being calm, and he never looked gloomy, his mind being joyous." To everyone Chuck met on his pilgrimage—professors, nuns, judges, homeless people, and the countless strangers who picked him up hitchhiking across the country—he communicated a spirit of freedom and responsibility and the thought that it would not be such a difficult thing, after all, to live by one's ideals.

Inspired, in part, by Chuck's example, I took a leave from college and made my way to the Catholic Worker in New York City to work with Dorothy Day. There in the following years our paths frequently coincided. While he revered Dorothy Day, his spiritual sensibility was closer to that of the Quakers, a matter of heeding the "inner voice" and tending to the "Seed of God" in his own soul and in others. In fact, Chuck avoided religious labels, declining even to call himself a Christian. Nevertheless he lived more consistently by the Sermon on the Mount than anyone I ever knew.

Over time Chuck's peacemaking energies turned to the field of alternative economics. He wanted to translate the principles of nonviolence into programs that would make a real difference in the lives of the poor. To that end he established investment funds, land trusts, and other programs that benefited countless poor families and struggling communities. (For someone who continued to live at a subsistence level, he showed a positive genius for financial management.) No matter what the task or the challenge he always brought his full energy. As his mother later said, "His life was his work, and his work was his life."

Now that life was ending. After a long battle with thyroid cancer and no longer able to eat or talk, he had refused further treatment and returned to his home in rural Connecticut to die. When I heard this news, I hastened to see him, uncertain what to expect or how we would communicate. When I arrived the next day, I found him seated in a wheelchair with a computer poised on his lap. He looked very old and frail, though the familiar spirit was there in his eyes and in the words he tapped out weakly on his keyboard.

I was ashamed to have been so out of touch during his

illness, but Chuck swept that aside. "We have both been occupied, appropriately so," he typed, "but now you are here."

After catching up on news, I described the book I was writing. I told him I was trying to explore, through the lives of holy people, what makes for a whole and happy life.

"I have a lot of thoughts about this," he wrote. "Would you like me to share them with you?" I said indeed I would. And so he began typing away.

"Since I got sick many people have asked whether I am angry, frustrated, bitter. And I say, 'Never.' When people receive the diagnosis of a terminal illness they are first of all afraid of being alone, and they wonder about how they might have lived differently. But I have never been alone. I have been surrounded by good friends and community, and I have been blessed with meaningful work. I have never had to make decisions on the basis of money or peer pressure. Of course looking back there are things I would do differently. If it were otherwise it would mean that I had not learned from life."

He acknowledged that it was tempting sometimes to be discouraged. "You know how Dorothy wrote in the postcript to *The Long Loneliness* about how hard it is to remember 'the duty of delight.' But as I contemplate the life I had and the end that is coming, I think: 'It's not so hard, either, when one has been graced by such good work and good friends.' To me it is the recognition that we are never without a meaningful choice. This is a culture that nearly drowns people with meaningless consumer choices, yet leaves most of them feeling that they are powerless in the most important affairs of life—but that's not true."

I was sitting at his side, reading the words as they appeared on the screen of his laptop computer. He paused occasionally, sometimes backing up and correcting a word that was not right. He was terribly weak. And then, echoing the subject of our first conversation, he continued: "We may not be able to choose the moment of our entry into the world, the circumstances that confront us, the choices available, or the consequences that face us for making them. But we can always decide *how* we will respond. . . . We can keep hold of the only 'possession' that cannot be taken from us: our dignity, integrity, soul, call-it-what-you-will. That is the decision that defines us, the first important 'life lesson' we should teach our children."

He was thinking of his niece and nephews.

"This is the decision I have to make every morning: I can rise and think about what has been done to me, what I have lost . . . or I can rise and say to myself, 'Here I am. Let's get moving!' With gratitude for good work, good friends, and a wonderful family, it's not a hard choice to make. . . . It's not hard to remember the 'duty of delight.' "

The conversation drifted on until late in the day, when the autumn sun began to wane. Overall he kept expressing his general satisfaction with life, and the absence of regrets. "Dostoevsky wrote that every age has need of a few fools," he noted.

I was reminded of the scene in the *Confessions* where St. Augustine described his final conversation with his mother about the happiness of the saints. In our case, however, the topic had not led us to the ethereal heights of heaven but to the ordinary realm of family, friends, and work. Still, I was aware, as we said good-bye, that I had been in the presence of a great soul, someone who had in his own way found the whole and happy life I had been struggling to describe.

Driving home, I could not help following the thread of my life back to the holy dreams and desires of my youth, when, along with Chuck, I had spurned the "deadness" of the world and set off to find the meaning of life. Twenty-eight years later I was still seeking what he had found. And as I drove through the night, I thought about my wife and my sleeping children, and of the work to be done, and of the duty of delight.

✦

Of the saints discussed in this book, many stood out among their contemporaries for their moral heroism, their charity, their zeal for God, or their genius in the spiritual life. There is a danger, in focusing on these exceptional lives, that their sacrifice, vision, or simple goodness will seem so far beyond our capacities as to render them worthless as guides. Dorothy Day was sensitive to this danger. "When they call you a saint," she used to say, "it means basically that you are not to be taken seriously."

But among history's vast company of holy people, the canonized saints represent only a small portion. Most saints remained anonymous and unrecognized, apart from their neighbors or their immediate family. Some of them were brilliant; others, simple. All of them struggled to achieve the "one thing necessary," to conform their lives to the pattern of the gospel, whatever the cost.

In *Middlemarch*, George Eliot bracketed her story about provincial Victorian society, surprisingly, with a meditation on St. Teresa of Ávila. By way of contrast with this passionate saint, "whose ideal nature demanded an epic life," Eliot offered a wry comment on her novel's largehearted heroine,

Dorothea Brooke, "offspring of a certain spiritual grandeur ill-matched with the meanness of opportunity." Dorothea's fate, apparently, was to live in a time and place that offered no material or occasion to express her potential greatness.

But her story was not a tragedy. Unlike St. Teresa, Dorothea may be the "foundress of nothing." Still, Eliot intended to portray her stumbling efforts to lead a good life as constituting her own kind of heroism. Eliot concluded the novel with this estimation: "Her full nature, like that river of which Cyrus broke the strength, spent itself in channels which had no great name on the earth. But the effect of her being on those around her was incalculably diffusive, for the growing good of the world is partly dependent on unhistoric acts, and that things are not so ill with you and me as they might have been is half owing to the number who lived faithfully a hidden life and rest in unvisited tombs."

If the canonized saints are the prodigies of the spiritual life, not everyone is called to be a prodigy. Founders and foundresses of nothing, we may express our holiness in unhistoric acts of kindness and compassion. But in walking this path, worn smooth by the steps of so many other saints, we find ourselves on the way of happiness. It is not the happiness of a storybook ending, for there is in all our happiness the promise of something larger and greater, that ending that alone justifies the hope of "living happily ever after." Nevertheless, each of the "lessons" in this book offers an entry point to that journey. Some will travel far. Others hardly at all. But like any great enterprise, this journey always begins with the first step.

NOTES

Preface

On saints: The best reference remains *Butler's Lives of the Saints*, edited by Herbert Thurston, S.J., and Donald Attwater, available in four volumes from Christian Classics, Inc. (Westminster, Md.: reprinted 1980). A new twelve-volume edition, edited by Paul Burns, is published by the Liturgical Press (Collegeville, Minn.: 1995–2000). Richard McBrien's *Lives of the Saints* (San Francisco: HarperSanFrancisco, 2001) offers a reliable one-volume reference, including helpful essays on the history and process of canonization. For a classic example of traditional hagiography, see Jacobus de Voragine, *The Golden Legend: Readings on the Saints*, trans. William Granger Ryan, 2 vols. (Princeton: Princeton University Press, 1993). Kenneth L. Woodward's *Making Saints* (New York: Simon & Schuster, 1990) offers a fascinating and entertaining study of "How the Catholic Church Determines Who Becomes a Saint, Who Doesn't, and Why." Most of the figures discussed in this book, along with many more, are also treated in my previous work *All Saints: Daily Reflections on Saints, Prophets, and Witnesses for Our Time* (New York: Crossroad, 1997).

ix Pascal, "The reason why": no. 148, *Pensées*, trans. A. J. Krailsheimer (New York: Penguin Books, 1966), 74.

ix St. Augustine on 288 schools of thought: trans. Henry Bettenson, in *The City of God*, Book 14:1 (New York: Penguin Books, 1972), 844.

xi Aristotle on happiness: See Book 1 of the *Nicomachean Ethics*. For a commentary, see Jean Vanier, *Made for Happiness: Discovering the Meaning of Life with Aristotle* (London: Darton, Longman, and Todd, 2001).

xi On happiness in the Beatitudes: I am grateful to Jim Forest for his discussion in *The Ladder of the Beatitudes* (Maryknoll, N.Y.: Orbis Books, 1999), 17–20.

xiv St. John of the Cross on the appetite for spiritual books: *The Dark Night of the Soul* (New York: Doubleday/Image, 1959), 44.

xv Jesus' words to Martha of Bethany: Luke 10:41–42.

xvi Thomas Merton, " 'one thing necessary' ": *No Man Is an Island* (New York: Doubleday/Image, 1967), 106, 107.

xvi Dorothy Day, "What's it all about—the Catholic Worker Movement?": "On Pilgrimage," *Catholic Worker* (March–April 1975). See Robert Ellsberg, ed., *Dorothy Day: Selected Writings* (Maryknoll, N.Y.: Orbis Books, 1992), 354.

xviii For the story of Jesus and the "rich young man": Mark 10:17–22 and parallels.

1: *Learning to Be Alive*

3 The epigraph from Serapion of Thmuis, "We beg you," is cited in Margaret Miles, *Fullness of Life: Historical Foundations for a New Asceticism* (Philadelphia: Westminster Press, 1981), 33.

4 William Blake, "priests in black gowns," from "The Garden of Love."

4 Jesus on "life in abundance": John 10:10.

4 St. Theophanis the Monk: *The Philokalia*, vol. 3 (London: Faber and Faber, 1984), 67.

4 St. Irenaeus, "The glory of God" ("*Gloria Dei vivens homo*"): *Against Heresies*.

5 George Orwell, "Saints should always be judged guilty": "Reflections on Gandhi," *The Penguin Essays of George Orwell* (New York: Penguin Books, 1968), 465.

6 Dorothy Day on the eating habits of saints: *On Pilgrimage* (Grand Rapids: William B. Eerdmans, 1999), 100.

6 Pierre Teilhard de Chardin, "zest for living": in *Pierre Teilhard de Chardin: Essential Writings*, ed. Ursula King (Maryknoll, N.Y.: Orbis Books), 128.

6 Thomas Merton, on sanctity as being "more fully human": *Life and Holiness* (New York: Doubleday/Image, 1964), 24.

7 Walker Percy, "The search": *The Moviegoer* (New York: Ballantine, 1988), 9.

7 Thomas Merton, "What I had abandoned": *Conjectures of a Guilty Bystander* (New York: Doubleday/Image, 1968), 46.

8 Henry David Thoreau, "To be awake is to be alive": *Walden* (New York: New American Library, 1960), 65.

8 On the desert fathers: Aside from the texts cited below, there are numerous sources, including Owen Chadwick, ed., *Western Asceticism* (Philadelphia: Westminster, 1958), and John Cassian, *The Conferences* (New York: Newman Press, 1997). There were also "desert mothers," though sadly, little record of their teachings is preserved. In this respect, Laura Swann's *The Forgotten Desert Mothers* (New York: Paulist Press, 2001) makes a valuable contribution.

9 For the stories of St. Simeon and St. Macarius: *Butler's Lives of the Saints*.

10 St. Antony, "My book is the nature of created things": Helen Waddell, trans., *The Desert Fathers* (New York: Vintage, 1998), 133.

10 Athanasius, *The Life of Antony*, trans. Robert C. Gregg (New York: Paulist Press, 1980). "His soul being free": 81.

11 St. Augustine's response to the life of St. Antony is related in Book 8 of his *Confessions*, trans. R. S. Pine-Coffin (New York: Penguin, 1961), 169.

12 Thomas Merton's reaction to asceticism: *The Seven Storey Mountain* (New York: Image, 1970), 227.

13 Merton's reflections on the desert fathers: the introduction to his anthology *The Wisdom of the Desert* (New York: New Directions, 1960), 5–6.

13 Merton, "If what most people take for granted": *Seven Storey Mountain*, 12. "What a strange thing": ibid., 203. "What wonderful happiness": ibid., 382.

15 James Martin's memoir: *In Good Company: The Fast Track from the Corporate World to Poverty, Chastity, and Obedience* (Franklin, Wis.: Sheed & Ward, 2000), 59–68.

17 " 'Why not be totally changed into fire?' ": Merton, *Wisdom of the Desert*, 50.

18 St. Antony, "The Fathers of old went forth": Waddell, *Desert Fathers*, 155.

18 Thoreau, "I left the woods": *Walden*, 214. His reflection on the "beautiful bug" appears on the last page of his "Conclusion," 22.

2: Learning to Let Go

23 Evagrius Ponticus (345–399), an early desert father and writer on ascetical spirituality, is the author of *The Praktikos*, from which his words on "a demon of sadness" are taken. *The Praktikos & Chapters on Prayer*, trans. John Eudes Bamberger, O.C.S.O. (Kalamazoo, Mich.: Cistercian Publications, 1978), 21. For texts by the desert fathers and mothers, see the references above.

23 Abba Moses, "those 'who have given away worldly wealth' ": John Cassian, *The Conferences*, Conference 3, ch. X, 129–30.

24 St. Serapion, "I have sold the book": Thomas Merton, *Wisdom of the Desert*, 37.

24 St. Antony, "Those who are not satisfied": *The Philokalia*, vol. I (London: Faber and Faber, 1979), 337.

25 On St. Francis of Assisi: The earliest biography is by Thomas of Celano, *St. Francis of Assisi*, trans. Placid Hermann, O.F.M.: (Chicago: Franciscan Herald Press, 1963). Classic stories from his life are found in *The Little Flowers of St. Francis*, trans. Raphael Brown (New York: Image, 1958). A concise selection of some of these early sayings is found in Stephen Clissold, *The Wisdom of St. Francis and His Companions* (New York: New Directions, 1978). The complete writings of St. Francis are available in *Francis and Clare: The Complete Writings*, trans. Regis J. Armstrong, O.F.M. Cap., and Ignatius C. Brady, O.F.M. (New York: Paulist Press, 1982). There are numerous recent biographies of St. Francis, including Adrian House, *Francis of Assisi: A Revolutionary Life* (New York: Paulist Press, 2001).

27 Brother Masseo, "Why you?": *Little Flowers of St. Francis*, 62.

28 A cardinal (John of Colonna), "This man merely wishes": Johannes
Jörgensen, *St. Francis of Assisi* (Garden City, N.Y.: Image, 1955), 85.

28 The bishop of Assisi to Francis: Clissold, *Wisdom of St. Francis*, 32.

29 Francis, "You are love, charity": Regis J. Armstrong, *St. Francis of Assisi: Writings for a Gospel Life* (New York: Crossroad, 1994), 202.

29 Carlo Carretto's words on St. Francis: *I, Francis* (Maryknoll, N.Y.: Orbis Books, 1982) and Robert Ellsberg, ed., *Carlo Carretto: Selected Writings* (Maryknoll, N.Y.: Orbis Books, 1994), 111.

30 Dorothy Day, "I have 'kissed a leper' ": *Dorothy Day: Selected Writings*, 110.

30 Thomas à Kempis, "every created thing will become for you a mirror": *The Imitation of Christ*, trans. Leo Sherley-Price (New York: Penguin, 1952), 72.

30 St. Augustine: His reflections on happiness appear throughout the *Confessions*. Otherwise the theme runs through most of his significant work, from his first book, *On the Happy Life*, through *City of God*, one of his last. The quote "Everyone . . . desires to be happy" is from Sermon 306:3. His reflections on "inordinate" love appear in several works, particularly in *On Christian Doctrine*. For a fresh look at his life, see Garry Wills, *Saint Augustine* (New York: Viking Penguin, 1999). Augustine's conversion is recounted in Book 8 of the *Confessions*. "Happiness is": ibid., 228.

34 St. Catherine of Genoa (1447–1510) was the author of a mystical classic, *Purgation and Purgatory*, available in the Paulist Press *Classics of Christian Spirituality* series. Her life and writings are the subject of a landmark work by Baron Friedrich von Hügel, *The Mystical Element of Religion* (New York: Crossroad, rep., 1999). See also *Butler's Lives*.

3: Learning to Work

37 The story of Abba Paul: Waddell, *Desert Fathers*, 166.

39 Leo Tolstoy's tale "A Talk Among Leisured People": *Walk in the Light and Twenty-three Tales* (Maryknoll, N.Y.: Orbis Books, 2003). Tolstoy described his own spiritual journey in *Confessions*, trans. David Patterson (New York: W. W. Norton, 1983).

42 Meister Eckhart, "To be right": *Meister Eckhart: A Modern Translation*, trans. Raymond B. Blackney (New York: Harper & Row, 1941), 11.

42 *The Rule of St. Benedict*, trans. Anthony C. Meisel and M. L. del Mastro (New York: Image Books, 1975). A good commentary on the rule can be found in Joan Chittister, *The Rule of St. Benedict: Insights for the Ages* (New York: Crossroad, 1993).

43 Brother Lawrence of the Resurrection, *The Practice of the Presence of God* (New York: Flemming Revell, 1958). "The time of business": 29. "Our sanctification": 23.

45 The cited hymn is "I Sing a Song of the Saints of Old," found in the Episcopal hymnal.

45 Meister Eckhart, "The kind of work": *Meister Eckhart*, 6.

46 Gerard Manley Hopkins on work and holiness: *Gerard Manley Hopkins: The Major Works*, ed. Catherine Phillips (Oxford: Oxford University Press, 1986). For Hopkins's idea of selving: Margaret Ellsberg, *Created to Praise: The Language of Gerard Manley Hopkins* (Oxford: Oxford University Press: 1987).

46 For Thomas Merton's reflections on the Shakers: Merton, *In Search of Paradise: The Spirit of the Shakers*, ed. Paul M. Pearson (Maryknoll, N.Y.: Orbis Books, 2003).

46 St. Christopher, see *Butler's Lives*.

48 Hopkins, "As kingfishers catch fire": *Gerard Manley Hopkins: The Major Works*, 129.

48 Merton's remark "A tree gives glory": Merton, *New Seeds of Contemplation* (New York: New Directions, 1961), 29.

49 Charles de Foucauld on vocation: *Charles de Foucauld: Selected Writings*, ed. Robert Ellsberg (Maryknoll, N.Y.: Orbis Books, 1999), 70.

49 Merton, "If we find": *No Man Is an Island*, 107.

50 Dorothy Day told the story of her early life and conversion in *The Long Loneliness* (New York: Harper & Row, 1952). "But there was another question": Dorothy Day: *Selected Writings*, 15. The best short biography is by Jim Forest, *Love Is the Measure* (Maryknoll, N.Y.: Orbis Books, 1993), now supplemented by Rosalie Riegle, *Dorothy Day: Portraits by Those Who Knew Her* (Maryknoll, N.Y.: Orbis Books, 2003).

54 For the story of Mother Teresa: *Mother Teresa of Calcutta: Essential Writings*, ed. Jean Maalouf (Maryknoll, N.Y.: Orbis Books, 2001). There are several comprehensive biographies. One of the best is by Kathryn Spink: *Mother Teresa: A Complete Authorized Biography* (San Francisco: HarperSanFrancisco, 1998).

55 Victor Frankl, *Man's Search for Meaning* (New York: Pocket Books, 1963), 122.

56 On Ita Ford: Judith M. Noone, *The Same Fate as the Poor* (Maryknoll, N.Y.: Orbis Books, 1995). Romero quote: ibid., 7. "This is a terrible time": 116.

57 Eckhart, "Doing the next thing": cited by Donald Nicholl, *Holiness* (London: Darton, Longman and Todd, 1981), 106.

58 Pierre Teilhard de Chardin, "God, in all that is most living": *The Divine Milieu* (New York: Harper & Row, 1965), 64.

4: Learning to Sit Still

59 On the Kingdom of Bhutan: Orville Schell, "Gross National Happiness," *Red Herring* (January 15, 2002).

62 Pascal: All quotations from *Pensées*. See "Diversion," 66–72. "God alone is man's true good": 75.

67 The Buddhist sutra "On Knowing the Better Way to Live Alone," along with commentary: Thich Nhat Hanh, *Our Appointment with Life: Discourse on Living Happily in the Present Moment* (Berkeley, Calif.: Parallax Press, 1990).

68 *The Philokalia* is available in English in three volumes, trans. G. E. H. Palmer, Philip Sherrard, and Kallistos Ware (London: Faber and Faber, 1979, 1981, 1984). Editors' note, 13.

69 *The Way of a Pilgrim and The Pilgrim Continues His Way*, trans. R. M. French (New York: Harper & Brothers, 1952).

70 Thich Nhat Hanh on "the present": *Thich Nhat Hanh: Essential Writings*, ed. Robert Ellsberg (Maryknoll, N.Y.: Orbis Books, 2001), 41.

71 Jean-Pierre de Caussade, *Abandonment to Divine Providence*, trans. John Beevers (New York: Image, 1975). The "mustard seed": 25. Faith: 37.

73 St. Benedict on "gyratory monks": *The Rule of St. Benedict*, 47.

74 Evagrius Ponticus on acedia: *Praktikos & Chapters on Prayer*, 18–19.

75 "When [acedia] besieges the unhappy mind," in Waddell, *The Desert Fathers*, 163–64.

75 Merton's restlessness is evident in his collected journals, particularly *A Search for Solitude*, vol. 3, *1952–1960*, ed. Lawrence S. Cunningham (New York: HarperCollins, 1996).

76 Evagrius, "When we meet": *Praktikos*, 23.

77 On the life of St. Catherine of Siena: Carol Lee Flinders, *Enduring Grace* (San Francisco: HarperSanFrancisco, 1993).

5: Learning to Love

79 William Blake, "to bear the beams of love": "The Little Black Boy," *Blake: Complete Writings* (Oxford: Oxford University Press, 1966), 125.

82 St. Augustine, "What do I love": *Confessions*, Book 10:6, 211. "In those days": 72.

83 Dorothy Day describes her relationship with Forster and the birth of their daughter in *The Long Loneliness*, in the section titled "Natural Happiness."

86 Sigmund Freud's reflections on love and happiness: *Civilization and Its Discontents*, trans. James Strachy (New York: W. W. Norton, 1962). 29. "A love that does not discriminate seems to me to forfeit a part of its own value, by doing an injustice to its object; and secondly, not all men are worthy of love": 49.

87 Mother Teresa, "God has identified himself": *Mother Teresa of Calcutta: Essential Writings*, ed. Maalouf, 47.

88 Freud, "We are never so helplessly unhappy": *Civilization*, 29.

88 Thomas Merton, "A happiness that is sought for ourselves alone": Merton, *No Man Is an Island* (Garden City, N.Y.: Doubleday, 1955), 17.

88 Charles Dickens, *A Christmas Carol* (New York: Dover, 1993), 66.

90 Fyodor Dostoevsky, "They wanted to say something": *Crime and Punishment*, trans. David Magarshack (New York: Penguin Books, 1966), 557.

91 Georges Bernanos, "Hell is not to love anymore": *Diary of a Country Priest*, trans. Pamela Morris (Garden City, N.Y.: Doubleday, 1954), 127.

91 St. Teresa of Ávila, "God and the soul," and "My Lord, I do not ask": Tessa Bielecki, *Teresa of Ávila: Mystical Writings* (New York: Crossroad, 1994), 156–57.

92 Fyodor Dostoevsky's Father Zossima: Dostoevsky, *The Brothers Karamazov*, trans. David Magarshack (New York: Penguin, 1958), 61–63.

93 St. Theophan the Recluse: *The Art of Prayer* (London: Faber & Faber, rep. 1997), 271.

93 St. Thérèse of Lisieux: *The Autobiography of St. Thérèse of Lisieux: The Story of a Soul*, trans. John Beevers (Garden City, N.Y.: Doubleday, 1957). See also Mary Frohlich, ed., *St. Therese of Lisieux: Essential Writings* (Maryknoll, N.Y.: Orbis Books, 2003). For a biography of St. Thérèse, see Monica Furlong, *Thérèse of Lisieux* (Maryknoll, N.Y.: Orbis Books, 2001).

96 For Dorothy Day's comments: *Therese* (Springfield, Ill.: Templegate, 1960). Selections also appear in Robert Ellsberg, ed., *Dorothy Day: Selected Writings*. "What kind of saint": 189. "The burden gets too heavy": *Selected Writings*, 219.

98 Thomas Merton, the monastery as "a school where we learn to be happy": in *The Seven Storey Mountain*, 451.

98 Tolstoy, "Happy families are all alike; every unhappy family is unhappy in its own way." The first sentence of *Anna Karenina*.

99 Day, "We cannot love God": *The Long Loneliness*, 285.

100 Engelmar Unzeitig's story: Adalbert Ludwig Balling and Reinhard Ablen, *Martyr of Brotherly Love: Father Engelmar Unzeitig and the Priests' Barracks at Dachau* (New York: Crossroad, 1992).

6: *Learning to Suffer*
104 Boethius's quotations: Boethius, *The Consolation of Philosophy*, trans. Richard Green (Indianapolis: Bobbs-Merrill, 1962).

106 Meister Eckhart, *The Book of Divine Comfort: Meister Eckhart: A Modern Translation*, trans. Raymond B. Blackney (New York: Harper & Row, 1941), 43–73.

109 Thomas of Celano, *St. Francis of Assisi*. Franciscan Herald Press, 1963).

110 St. Ignatius Loyola: *The Autobiography of St. Ignatius Loyola with Related Documents*, ed. John Olin (New York: Harper & Row, 1974), 21–26.

112 Julian of Norwich, *Showings*, trans. James Walsh, S.J. (New York: Paulist Press, 1978).

115 Leon Bloy, "In his poor heart": *Pilgrim of the Absolute*, ed. Raissa Maritain (New York: Pantheon, 1947), 349.

115 Ignatius, The *Spiritual Exercises*, trans. Anthony Mottola (Garden City, N.Y.: Image/Doubleday, 1964), 47.

115 Diadochos of Photiki, "As wax cannot take the imprint": *The Philokalia*, vol. 1, 291.

116 Pierre Teilhard de Chardin, "The lives of the saints": in *Pierre Teilhard de Chardin: Essential Writings*, ed. King, 87. His writing on passive diminishment appears in *The Divine Milieu* (New York: Harper & Row, 1965), 74–93. For an account of his life: Ursula King, *Spirit of Fire: The Life and Vision of Teilhard de Chardin* (Maryknoll, N.Y.: Orbis Books, 1996).

117 Quotations by Flannery O'Connor are taken from her published letters, *The Habit of Being*, ed. Sally Fitzgerald (New York: Farrar, Straus & Giroux, 1979). These texts also appear in *Flannery O'Connor: Spiritual Writings*, ed. Robert Ellsberg (Maryknoll, N.Y.: Orbis, 2003). For an insightful treatment of O'Connor's life and work (along with Thomas Merton, Dorothy Day, and Walker Percy): Paul Elie, *The Life You Save May Be Your Own: An American Pilgrimage* (New York: Farrar, Straus & Giroux, 2003).

121 Caussade, "to carry on as you are doing": *Abandonment to Divine Providence*, 35.

122 Sheila Cassidy's memoir: *Audacity to Believe* (London: Collins, 1977). "Do with me what you will" is from her later book *Sharing the Darkness: The Spirituality of Caring* (Maryknoll, N.Y.: Orbis Books, 1991).

124 Walter Ciszek wrote two accounts of his experience. *With God in Russia* (Garden City, N.Y.: Doubleday, 1964) is a straightforward autobiography; *He Leadeth Me* (Garden City, N.Y.: Doubleday, 1973) deals more with the spiritual lessons of his experience. The quotations here are from his later book.

127 St. Augustine, "You were guiding me as a helmsman": *Confessions*, Book 3:14.

128 Carlo Carretto described his experience in *Why O Lord* (Maryknoll, N.Y.: Orbis Books, 1986). See also *Carlo Carretto: Selected Writings*, ed. Robert Ellsberg (Maryknoll, N.Y.: Orbis Books, 1994).

131 Henri Nouwen's story is found in some of his published journals, including *Genesee Diary, ¡Gracias!, The Road to Daybreak*, and *Sabbatical Journey*. Biographical accounts are available in Robert Jonas's introduction to *Henri Nouwen: Selected Writings* (Maryknoll, N.Y.: Orbis Books, 1998) and Michael Ford's *Wounded Prophet* (New York: Doubleday, 1999). Nouwen described some of his experiences at L'Arche, including his experience of emotional breakdown, in *Adam: God's Beloved* (Maryknoll: Orbis Books, 1997) and in *The Inner Voice of Love* (New York: Doubleday, 1996). On the intermingling of sor-

row and joy: *Can You Drink the Cup?* (Notre Dame, Ind.: Ave Maria Press, 1996).

134 St. Augustine, *City of God* contains a long inventory of the forms of human suffering in Book 22:22.

135 Thomas à Kempis, *The Imitation of Christ*, Book 2, ch. 12: "On the Royal Road of the Holy Cross."

7: *Learning to Die*

138 St. Augustine, "From the moment a person begins to exist": *Confessions*, Book 13:10.

138 Pascal, "Being unable to cure death": *Pensées*, No. 133.

138 Leo Tolstoy, "The Death of Ivan Ilyich," *The Great Short Works of Leo Tolstoy*, trans. Louise and Aylmer Maude (New York: Harper & Row, 1967), 280.

140 Dietrich Bonhoeffer, "This is the end": J. Martin Bailey and Douglass Gilbert, *The Steps of Bonhoeffer* (New York: Macmillan, 1969), 73.

141 *Markings*, trans. Leif Sjöberg and W. H. Auden (New York: Alfred A. Knopf, 1964), 180.

142 Dietrich Bonhoeffer, "As we embark upon discipleship," appears in *The Cost of Discipleship*. See also *Dietrich Bonhoeffer: Essential Writings*, ed. Robert Coles (Maryknoll, N.Y.: Orbis Books, 1998), 61.

144 Thomas Merton's description of a postulant at Gethsemani appears in *The Seven Storey Mountain*, 394.

145 St. Augustine, "Don't leave us!" *Confessions*, 175–76.

146 Henri Nouwen's last year is chronicled in *Sabbatical Journey* (New York: Crossroad, 1998). The story of his accident and near-death experience is described in *Beyond the Mirror* (New York: Crossroad, 1992). His reflections on death and dying, including his reference to the Flying Rodleighs, appear in *Our Greatest Gift* (San Francisco: HarperCollinsSanFrancisco, 1994). Nouwen described his relationship with Adam in *Adam: God's Beloved* (Maryknoll: Orbis Books, 1997). His words "Many friends and family members have died . . ." appear at the end of *The Inner Voice of Love* (New York: Doubleday, 1996), 118.

152 Donald Nicholl's reflections: in *The Testing of Hearts: A Pilgrim's Journey*, rev. ed. (London: Darton, Longman and Todd, 1998).

153 Father Alfred Delp's reflections: *The Prison Meditations of Father Al-*

fred Delp (New York: Herder and Herder, 1963). A reprint is forthcoming: *Alfred Delp: Prison Writings* (Maryknoll, N.Y.: Orbis Books, 2004).

153 Flannery O'Connor's story "A Good Man Is Hard to Find": *Flannery O'Connor: The Complete Stories* (New York: Farrar, Straus & Giroux, 1971). The quotations cited here appear in *Flannery O'Connor: Spiritual Writings* (Maryknoll, N.Y.: Orbis Books, 2003).

154 Thomas à Kempis, "A Meditation on Death": *The Imitation of Christ*, Book 1, ch. 23.

155 Quote from the author of *The Cloud of Unknowing*: "The Epistle of Prayer," published as an appendix to his more famous work. See *The Cloud of Unknowing and Other Works* (New York: Penguin, 1961).

158 Martin Luther King's account of his "vision in the kitchen," along with his speech in Memphis: James Cone's *Martin & Malcolm & America: A Dream or a Nightmare* (Maryknoll, N.Y.: Orbis Books, 1991), 124–25. See also Martin Luther King, *Strength to Love* (Philadelphia: Fortress Press, 1981), 113.

163 Joseph Cardinal Bernardin's *The Gift of Peace* (Chicago: Loyola Press, 1997) was published after his death. "It is quite clear": 151.

166 The conversion of King Edwin: Bede, *A History of the English Church and People*, trans. Leo Sherley-Price (New York: Penguin, 1955), Book 2, ch. 13, 125.

167 The story of Henri Nouwen's lecture at Yale is recounted by Fred Bratman in Beth Porter, ed., *Befriending Life: Encounters with Henri Nouwen* (New York: Doubleday, 2001), 247.

8: Learning to See

170 Dante's description of the Beatific Vision: *The Divine Comedy*, vol. 3, *Paradiso*, Canto 33; this translation is by Mark Musa (Bloomington: Indiana University Press, 1984), 394. For other literary treatments of heaven, see *The Book of Heaven*, eds. Carol Zaleski and Philip Zaleski (New York: Oxford University Press, 2000).

171 Hopkins, "the dearest freshness deep down things": "God's Grandeur."

171 Augustine's words on the "eyes of the heart": "Commentary" on the Sermon on the Mount," Book 1:8.

172 Thomas Aquinas's treatise on happiness: *Summa Theologica* Ia IIae Q 1–5 (Westminster, Md.: Christian Classics, 1981), vol. 2, 583–615.

173 St. Augustine, "Suppose we were wanderers": *Christian Doctrine* (Indianapolis: Bobbs-Merrill, 1958), 9–10.

174 Dietrich Bonhoeffer, "I believe we ought so to love and trust God": *Letters and Papers from Prison* (New York: Macmillan, 1972), 267.

175 Aquinas, "Men esteem that there is some kind of happiness": ibid., 611.

175 St. Catherine of Siena, "All the way to Heaven": frequently quoted by Dorothy Day.

176 Thomas Merton's remark about *The Seven Storey Mountain: The Sign of Jonas* (Garden City, N.Y.: Doubleday, 1956), 318. The account of his vision in Louisville: *Conjectures of a Guilty Bystander* (Garden City, N.Y.: Doubleday/Image, 1968), 156–58.

177 The story of the Transfiguration of Christ: Mark 9:28 and parallels.

178 Georges Bernanos, "I don't suppose": from *Diary of a Country Priest*, 129.

179 Brother Lawrence's vision: *The Practice of the Presence of God*, 11.

180 Augustine's conversation with his mother: *Confessions*, Book 9.

181 Dorothy Day's memory of Mrs. Barrett: *Dorothy Day: Selected Writings*, 11. "We are trying to make people happy": 102.

183 Augustine's reflections on the Beatific Vision: Book 22 of *City of God*.

184 Caussade, "Faith transforms the earth": *Abandonment to Divine Providence*, 37.

185 John Henry Newman's sermon on happiness and heaven: "Holiness Necessary for Future Blessedness," in John Henry Newman, *Selected Sermons, Prayers, and Devotions*, ed. John F. Thornton and Susan B. Varenne (New York: Vintage Books, 1999), 3–11.

188 Father Zossima's words: Dostoevsky, *The Brothers Karamazov*, vol. 1, 352.

188 Titus Brandsma's story: Woodward, *Making Saints*.

Conclusion

189 Merton, "I should have been a happy person": *The Seven Storey Mountain*, 12.

190 "Loveliness of the spirit": Eric Gill's definition of holiness.

190 "There is no way *to* happiness. But there is a way *of* happiness": I am grateful to David Anderson, author of *Breakfast Epiphanies* (Boston: Beacon Press, 2002), for suggesting this distinction.

191 The image of the "mental telescope": Leo Tolstoy, *War and Peace*, trans. Ann Dunnigan (New York: Penguin, 1968), 1320. After Pierre's

ordeal in prison he discarded his "mental telescope." Whereas before "he had been unable to see the great, the unfathomable, the infinite, in anything," now "he had learned to see the great, the eternal, the infinite in everything. . . . And the closer he looked, the happier and more serene he was."

191 On Chuck Matthei: I have written longer accounts of our last meeting for *Sojourners* magazine ("The Duty of Delight . . . and other lessons from a life well-lived" [January–February 2003]), and *The Catholic Worker* ("Chuck Matthei, 1948–2002" [January–February 2003]).

194 Dorothy Day on "the duty of delight": "I found myself, a barren woman, the joyful mother of children. It is not easy always to be joyful, to keep in mind the duty of delight." Postscript to *The Long Loneliness*, 285.

196 George Eliot, *Middlemarch* (Boston: Houghton Mifflin, 1956), 4, 613.

ACKNOWLEDGMENTS

THANKS to those friends and family members who read this work in earlier drafts, particularly Robert Jonas, Jim Forest, Wes-Howard Brook, Kerry Walters, Joan Chittister, my brother Michael, and my mother, Carol Cummings. Their critical comments were extremely helpful. Thanks to Phyllis Theroux and my agent, Molly Friedrich, faithful friends who accompanied me every step of the way. Special thanks to my colleague Michael Leach, who believed in this project even when I doubted. I am enormously grateful to my editor, Paul Elie, whose skills, learning, and spiritual preoccupations made him an ideal partner for this book. Thanks as well to everyone at Farrar, Straus and Giroux for their professionalism and enthusiasm.

I cannot list all the people who have supported me with their prayers, encouragement, and friendship, but I would especially like to acknowledge Daria Donnelly, Steve De-Mott, Rachelle Linner, Jim Martin, Kathy Boudin, Bernadette Price, and the late Chuck Matthei.

No words are adequate to thank my wife, Peggy, whose good influence shines through the better parts of this book as it otherwise does in my life. Final thanks go to our children, Nicholas, Catherine, and Christina: after the saints, my guides to happiness.

INDEX